HINDUISM
A SCIENTIFIC RELIGION

HINDUISM
A SCIENTIFIC RELIGION

& SOME TEMPLES IN SRI LANKA

PON KULENDIREN

iUniverse, Inc.
Bloomington

Hinduism a Scientific Religion
& Some Temples in Sri Lanka

iUniverse books may be ordered through booksellers or by contacting:

iUniverse
1663 Liberty Drive
Bloomington, IN 47403
www.iuniverse.com
1-800-Authors (1-800-288-4677)

ISBN: 978-1-4759-3673-5 (sc)
ISBN: 978-1-4759-3674-2 (hc)
ISBN: 978-1-4759-3675-9 (ebk)

Printed in the United States of America

iUniverse rev. date: 10/08/2012

CONTENTS

FOREWORD

It's a naked truth that Hinduism is the oldest and realistic religion, which emphasize the worship of the power full natures called (Energies) *'Sakthis'*. There are five natural elements called *'Pancha Poothangal'* which are water, wind, fire, earth & sky. According to Hinduism God is eternal, omnipotent and omnipresent in the form of *'sakthy'*. Eternal means no birth or death (*'Athi, Antham'*). So the authentic pre natives of India worshiped these five elements as God at the beginning. Later on, they invented the Sun as the route for all these five elements and started to worship the sun which called *'Sooriya Namaskaram'*.

Gradually when they developed knowledge, they drew the picture of an imaginary super powered character with four hands named *'Shiva'* bearing all those five elements and carved the statue too. Hinduism strictly forbidden sins (*'Pancha maa paathagangal'*), those are five bad things — telling lie, steeling, gambling, arguing and killing. "Every action has an opposite reaction" is the scientific law of dynamics invented very lately. But Hinduism specified in very ancient time the *'Karma,'* the action which we commit in this birth will react in the next birth. Next birth is designed on the basis of 'Karma'. Hinduism is the only religion mentioned about the rebirth and reincarnation, right from the beginning. Now day's scientists have accepted as there is rebirth. Also it's preached human beings should be strictly vegetarians. Later on this was proved scientifically the human's internal organs were designed to digest only the vegetables, not like carnivorous animals. Hinduism says killing of any lives even for meals is a sin. But all other religions say killing of any animals for food is not sinner.

Few people started to meditate for several hours and days by completely forget about themselves and the food called fasting '*Viratham*'. By doing so they gained extra ordinary knowledge and power called '*Gnanam*'. Through '*Ganam*' they had super vision and their soul could able to fly from one continent to another, cured the uncured chronic sick people and did many miracles. They were called as '*Grannies*' '*Trishies*' and '*Gurus*'. They wrote many worthy books about the basic principles and logics of the Hinduism called '*Vetham*', *Vethantham*', '*Upanidatham*' etc. Still there are many '*Gnanies*' doing meditation in the undisturbed caves in Himalaya mountain. Even though they were ordinary men they gained wide spiritual knowledge in order to find out the answers to their questions '*who am I, from where did*

I come and where will I go? That's the basic principle of the Hinduism—if a person I realized whom am I then he could able to realize the God. *'Gnanies'* could able to calculate the movements of the planets without any special equipments like the present days scientist uses and also predicted how it will affect the individuals—that process called *'Astrology'*.

Few *'Gurus'* shared their knowledge with their disciples and taught to them about Hinduism to become *'Gnanies'*. But in the mean time one particular group called *'Brahmanas'* (Brahmins) studied only the *'mantras'* in 'Sanskrit' language claimed themselves as *'Gurus'* and started to do *'Pooja'* in the temples for their living and compelled others to worship the idols in the temples and pay for them *'Thadchani'* (colly), with rice, vegetables and clothes to their services. They know nothing about Hinduism at all. Making money is their only motive as the author of this book Mr. Kulendiren pointed out.

The Gurus and disciple teaching system gradually vanished. The school teachers taught nothing about Hinduism but just the *Thaevaram, Thiruvasakam* and the life history of the *Samaya Kuravars* who sang those. So the current generation believes Hinduism is just the idol worship and gets satisfied by doing that from the birth till death. The Hindus think mistakenly that they are offering to the God and offering everything to the Brahmins. But not offer a penny to the poor people begging along the street. The Hinduism says "See the God from the smile of the poorest". The God is desire less at all (*'Ethilumae Patru Illaathavar'*), though love only the true love. Thiruvalluwar said in Kural # 350.

"Attach and tie thyself to Him who hath conquered all attachments: bind thyself firmly to him in order that all thy bonds may be broken".(Tamil translation:*'Patruka patru atraan patrinai patruka patru vidatku'.*

The author has touched on the importance of Energy in Hinduism. He diagrammatically explained how energy is applied to human living and nature and the scientific laws related to Energy.

But the philosophical thinker and well known writer Mr. Pon Kulendiren wrote this book "Hinduism is a Scientific Religion' in English at the right time to enlighten the younger generations of this twenty first century. I wish that he will write more and more books about Hinduism with deep conceptions.

Some years ago the author wrote in Tamil about Hinduism and at the request of many young people who wanted it to be in English, this book is written in English to touch on different aspects of science in Hinduism, and he focuses in this book on Nature, Energy and interpretation of idol worship in Hinduism, which the younger generation is keener in knowing. The book also covers the historical background of five Siva Temples

(Iswarams) in Sri Lanka and specific Murugan temples such as Nallur, Kathirgamam, and Maviddapuram

Buddhism also touches on Rebirth and Karma and is an offspring of Hinduism and it has link to Hinduism. In Sri Lanka, Buddhist Viharas contain Hindu idols like Vishnu, Ganapathy. Karthigeyan, and Pathini. I wish that the writer of this book will write more and more books about Hinduism with deep analysis of the religion for younger generation to understand.

Virakesari Moorthy
Writer, Author & Journalist
Mississauga, Ontario,
Canada — 12th June 2012

PREFACE

People encounter many problems in daily life and calls for God's help to resolve the issues. The issues are concerned with finance, education, family life, health, jobs etc and man seeks help from god to solve the problems. Temple is the place where god resides. The temple set up is a place of purity and it is the place where man finds peace. It is the place of trust and respect. Some temples are built with the motive of business. In Sri Lanka, names for many Hindu temples are given to cater for the people from certain locations. For the people who migrated to Canada, UK, and other countries, we cannot expect them to know the history of the temple. If you ask them who established the five Ishwarams in Lanka and the history behind them, they may not know. The people from Manipay village will know about Maruthadi Pillayar, Nallur people will know about Nallur Kandasamy kovil, Tellipalai will know about Mavidapuram, Thunalai village will know about Vallipuram temple. Devotees walk a long distance of about 300 miles in forty days, along the eastern coast of Sri Lanka, every year known as (Paatha Yathirai) and know about the importance of Kathirgamam.

Dravidians built the Gopuram of the temple are in a tall triangular shape, similar to Egyptian Pyramids. Gopurams have openings in odd numbers. The reason is to light a lamp in those holes to identify the presence of Gopuram. The Gopuram's origins can be traced back to early structures of the Pallavas and by the twelfth century under the Paandya rulers. Madurai Meenatchi Amman temple consists of 14 gopurams including two golden gopurams for the main deities. In an island like Nedunteevu people worship Rameshwaram by looking at the gopuram from far distance, across the sea, as the island is not too far from Rameshwaram.

There are many questions are raised by the younger generation about Hinduism. What is the concept of "Aum" in Hinduism? Why 108 is an important number in Hinduism? What is the purpose of rituals, mantras in Hinduism? What are the scientific explanations given about Hinduism?

In Lanka Hinduism and Buddhism exits and various idols are worshipped in the same worshiping location. One of the interesting questions are raised by the youth as to how could Hindu idols have more than two hands, and one head? One of the reasoning given is that main concept and functions of Hindu idols is represented by symbols. This is explained in this book. The typical example is the idol of Ganapathy. The appearance of the idol of god Gnash explains the philosophy of man's life. Meetings, gatherings, weddings, functions and celebrations begin with a prayer of lord Ganesh.

Hindus and Buddhists worship Shiva, Vishnu, Murugan (Karthigeyan), Kannagi, Ganapathy etc. The fundamental concept of Hinduism is based on cosmic energy and Nature. Birth, Life and Death referred to as Brahman, Vishnu and Shiva. Vedas are written many thousands of years ago, based on the decoding of the secrets of nature. It has developed through cultural relationship and legendary stories. Stories make people to understand the concepts. In Hinduism many legendary stories exist explaining the philosophy of human life.

Temples are built based on architectural concept (Vaastu sasthiram). Locations such as River banks, Sea coast, Mountains, forests, places where Yogis attained Samadhi, are selected for locating the temples. The suitable places are locations where vibrations exist. This establishes the respect Hinduism gives to nature. The vibrations generated from such locations are considered as ideal for locating the temples.

The contents of this book explain the science behind Hinduism and about important Hindu temples in Lanka. When Portuguese invaded Lanka, they destroyed many temples to establish Catholic religion and convert people's religion. Then Dutch took over and they spread

Christianity. Finally, the British concentrated on the administration and development of the country. Since the majority of the Lankans are Buddhists they focused on their religion. Muslims, through their migration to Lanka, developed Islam. When they invaded in India, they did tremendous damage to Hinduism.

There should not be corruption in the management of temples. It should not be treated as a business establishment. This book was first written in Tamil. At the request of many people it is translated to English with modifications, for the knowledge of the younger generation. Interesting questions are raised by youth about Hinduism, mainly about idol worship and rituals. This book, as far as possible answers some of the many questions youth have about Hinduism and the beliefs Hindus have. It gives the scientific explanation for the beliefs and procedures adopted in Hinduism. The book explains the significance of many temples in Sri Lanka which were built by the Tamil kings from South India and some rulers of Lanka and was subject to destruction by foreign invaders.

Pon Kulendiren
Writer, Journalist
Telecom Consultant
Mississauga, Ontario, Canada

1

Origin of Hinduism

"Religion is a culture of faith; Science is a culture of doubt." So said Richard Feynman, Nobel-prize-winning physicist

There is truth in this statement. Hinduism is built on faith and nature. Laws are formulated from the observation of happenings in nature. Different forms of energies, and parameters such as waves, vibration, that makes things to happen in nature, provide the explanation for beliefs in Hinduism.

Religion is a collection of cultural systems, beliefs, world views that establish symbols and relates humanity to spiruality and moral values. Books are written on each religion, tracing the history. Other than many religions, there are 21 major religions in the world. Christianity is the leading one by the number of people who follow, second being Islam, Hinduism being fourth. There are various divisions within Hinduism, but the basic concept is the same. Each Religion is like tributaries of a river flowing into a sea, reflecting the overall concept. Like the water in the main river, it carries the main philosophy for the human being to live. The water in the river called religion can be polluted, depending on the people using it for their purpose.

Since Sanskrit is the oldest written language, as far as religion being written down, and as far as organized religion is concerned, it would be Hinduism. Vedic books are written in Sanskrit and by Yogis through interaction with nature and understanding its secrets. Out of so many religions in the world, Hinduism is the oldest spiritual religion which had its origin in Indus Valley civilization area in Pakistan, one time part of India. If you ask about the origin of Hinduism to a person who has perceived the essence of Hinduism, the answer will be a simple smile. He will never give a definite reply as to the exact date of origin of Hinduism like Christianity, Islam, and Buddhism. The originator of Hinduism like the other religions is not known. Hinduism has no history, it believes in the present. This might be hard for a common man to digest because we live in a world, which gives so much importance to history, human life and avatars. Teachings of Hinduism focus on the way of life and human conduct.

Beginning of Hinduism is based on nature as such it involves scientific concepts just like Physics, Biology which comes out from the hidden secrets of nature. It also explains the creation, existence and destruction, the main three happenings in life, the main components of nature. Hinduism defined the names Brahma for creation, Vishnu for preservation or existence and Shiva for destruction. These three happenings takes place in a cycle and undergo purification of soul. As per Swami Vivekananda, the human soul is eternal and immortal, perfect and infinite. Death means only a change of center from one body to another. The present is determined by our past actions and the future by the present. The soul will go on evolving up or reverting back from birth to birth and death to death. The laws and explanations of happenings in the nature and discoveries based on what we see in nature from, the foundation of science. Furthermore, Hinduism's foundation is nature and the interpretation of GOD is based on nature and its behaviour. The three main activities in nature are the **BIRTH, GROWTH** and **DEATH** and this gets repeated over and over again in a cyclic form. In Hinduism it is termed reincarnation, assumed to be **a** process of purification of the soul.

Karma is basically energy and is associated with action whether good or bad. The energy of Karma is thrown out through thoughts, words and deeds, and it comes back to the responsible person in time, through other people. Karma is our best teacher, for we must

3

always face the consequences of our actions and thus improve and refine our behavior, or suffer if we do not. We Hindus look at time as a circle, as things cycle around again. Professor Einstein came to the same conclusion.

That is why for easy understanding of Hinduism, Hindu idols are built on the basis of family and relations, as a result, rituals are performed based on the processes. Body, Soul and Mind are important ingredients of Hinduism. We have to think before we act. We should have a body to act. When we act we use the body to produce good or bad results.

The great sages who gave us the Upanishads, Vedas and other Holy Scriptures, never talked about the history of their clan or kingdom. This is because history is of not much use to mankind. But the great thoughts found in Upanishads are eternal and have practical use in everyday life. They knew very well that history creates nothing but wars and tension. Mythological stories were created to make the devotees to understand the concepts. They believed in the stories and made them to understand the concepts.

Our world is dominated by monolithic religions. These religions have a proper beginning and founders. But Hinduism has no founders because simply it is not a religion but a way of life. It talks more about day-to-day problems. It deals with questions that every human being ask at sometime in life like 'Who am I?' Hinduism deals with self realization. It deals with Karma and reincarnation." What you saw is what you reap" is the fundamental concept of Karma. This concept wants human life to do good things and not to expect anything in return. Many of Hindu philosophies are preached in Bagawatt Geeta.

Other religions originated from Hinduism like tributaries of a main river. Although there is infighting between religions claiming supremacy over each other, this is because they fail to understand the inner secrets of their religion and misuse. Even within Hinduism there are various sects. The question of origin of Hinduism arises because other religions in the world have an origin. Modern education also might prompt a person to ask about the origin. So, many Hindus are forced to give a period of origin or a particular era and not a specific date.

There is an ongoing controversy over the origin of Hinduism. The traditional view is that Hinduism originated around 3000 BCE. But various modern scholars have challenged the 3000 BCE origin story. There is no proper historical record. They argue that Hindu religion originated somewhere between 3500 and 5000 BCE. The 5000 BCE origin story is backed by the findings from Indus Valley Civilization located in present day Pakistan and Afghanistan areas. These areas, due to Islamic invasion, became Muslim areas and Hindu and Buddhist cultures were destroyed. A typical example is the destruction of the more than 2000 year old Bamyan Buddha statue in the cave, by Talibans against idol worship. A link between Hinduism and Nature and hence life of all forms could be seen in Hindu temples. Nature is Science. Concepts and laws in Physics, Chemistry, Biology, Mathematics, and Astronomy are all derived from nature and the happenings in the nature. In Hinduism, Fire, Water, Earth, Space, and Ether are considered as five boothas (sources of energies) and are present in each and every ritual. Temples are built in India and worshiped for these five sources of energy. Different parts of the body do indeed have sympathetic frequencies. The natural frequency of the body is vital to think alike and act alike. It plays an important part in meditation. Yogis and Rishi had the ability to change their frequencies and hence read the mind of others.

When you go deeper and deeper into Hinduism, you will unearth many coded secrets of science. The Rishis through their powerful meditating power interacted with nature and discovered the secrets of it. The mantras were formed by them based on their findings. Chanting of the mantras provides more vibrational energy. The energy in the universe is the vital part of Hinduism and everything revolves around it. Planets including earth and other galaxies survive for its existence on energy. As time goes on new discoveries are made in Universe and new laws framed. It is that which could not be seen but the results could be felt in different forms. It exists in different forms in the same way Hinduism exists in different forms of idols and easy for ordinary human to understand energy. Beliefs, plays an important part in Hinduism.

The aspect in nature is the forces which could be attractive or repulsive, good or bad. Forces also play an important part in the creation of universe, along with energy. Forces have created disasters in nature such as tsunamis, earthquakes, floods, tornadoes and volcanoes. The outcome of these events is given explanation in Hinduism as outcome of the actions by Boomathevi (Earth), Varuna (Rain), and Agni (Fire). The five elements are basically the five states of matter. Earth refers to Solid; Water to Liquid, Air to gas, and Fire to plasma and Ether is referred as Empty space, also as a state of matter.

The names Devas and Yakkas were given in Hinduism for good and bad forces for easy understanding by people. The war between the two reflects the outcome of the forces. Legendary stories are written about the good and bad forces. A typical example is the stories of Ramayana, Mahabharata and other legendary stories. The stories teach a lesson to the people. "Bagawatt Gita" is the epic of the philosophical teachings from the Mahabharata war. The moral, social, and spiritual values are taught in the story of Ramayana. Upanishads are a collection of philosophical texts which form the theoretical basis of Hinduism. The "Thirukkural" treated as a 133 chapters that contains 1330 rhyming Tamil couplets of divine text, written in Tamilnadu that expounds on various aspects of life. These writings leads to the way human life should guide itself towards spiritualism and purify its birth.

2

Design of the Hindu Temple

It is estimated that that there are more than 4200 religions in the world out which the five leading ones are Christianity (2.1 billion), Islam(1.5 billion), Secular/Irreligious/Agnostic/Atheist 1.1 billion, Hinduism (1 billion), Buddhism (0.5 billion). To live happily in this world, we need to follow some basic concepts. The concepts may differ in religions but the aim is the same. People change religion for many reasons. Lack of understanding the concept is one of the main reasons to change religion. Getting some form of benefits by changing religion is another reason. This reason is evident from change in religions in Sri Lanka through forced conversion. In Hinduism science and nature are imbedded in it and many people are not aware of it. Religious rituals too are linked to nature and science

There is a popular proverb in Tamil language, which goes as *"Do not reside in a town where there is no Temple"*. The Hindu temple is termed **"Aalayam" or "Kovil"**.

What does that term means? How old is Hinduism? How should the Hindu temple, the worshiping place for Hindus like the church for Catholics and Christians, Dagoba for Buddhists and Mosques should be constructed? Of course there is a difference in the appearance of these worship places but the objective is the same, which is to find inner peace through worshiping by concentration of mind.

Aalayam means the place where GOD resides. Ko+vil = Ko means the leader or God and Vil means the place where one resides. Hence Kovil is the residing place of God, similar to the womb of the mother where fetus resides. The temple is the place where the distance between Man and God could be narrowed and that through meditation or worshiping. People when they get into the temple they normally sit and meditate for few minutes. A link is established between GOD and the Human soul. COSMOS is the place where GOD resides. Hence temple is a symbol of COSMOS. Cosmic Energy resides in COSMOS and hence GOD is a form of energy. The main objective of this good energy found in a Temple if properly constructed, liberates man from ignorance. It helps him to attain wisdom.

HINDUISM

Before we go further into the concept of Hindu temple we should know about the Hindu religion. According to historians, the origin of Hinduism dates back to 3,000 or more years. The word "Hindu" is derived from the name of the **river** INDUS or some times called SINDHU, a great Trans-Himalayan river. It is one of the longest rivers in the world with an astonishing length of 2900 km. Rising in south-western Tibet, at an altitude of 16,000 feet, Sindhu enters the Indian territory near Leh in Ladakh in a region in the Indian state of Jammu and Kashmir. The river has total drainage area of about 450,000 square miles, of which 175,000 square miles, lie in the Himalayan mountains and foothills. Sindhu river derived its name from Sanskrit language. It is mentioned in Rig Veda (1500 BC) and in the hymns of Aryan people of ancient India. The Aryans who invaded the area, gave the name Hindu to Sindhu river. This river became the cradle of Indus Valley civilization that existed before 1500BC. The civilization flourished along its banks and Vedas of Hinduism were born there. In the course of time the name "Indus" Hindu was given. The belief that Hinduism was brought to India by the Aryans is now considered flawed and treated as a myth. Aryans invaded the Indus valley and settled along the banks of Indus River. The Aryans were a tribe of

Indo-European-speaking, horse-riding nomads living in the arid steppes of Eurasia. Adolph Hitler twisted the theories of Gustaf Kossinna (1858-1931), to put forward the Aryans as a master race of Indo-Europeans, who were supposed to be Nordic in appearance and directly ancestral to the Germans. Persians who migrated to India called the Sindhu River 'Hindu', the land 'Hindustan' and its inhabitants 'Hindus'. According to scholars, the evolution of Hinduism may be divided into three periods: the ancient (6500 BCE-1000 AD), the medieval (1000-1800 AD), and the modern (1800 AD to present). Hinduism is commonly thought to be the oldest religion in the history of human civilization. The theory of Aryan invasion of Indus valley civilization is now considered as a myth and hence Aryans are not responsible for introducing Hinduism

Along the Jordan River Christianity, Islam and Judaism came up. Jordanism could become a modern word to name all three of these religions, which do have similar beliefs and practices. Along the banks of Sindhu River, Hinduism grew. There are four important surviving religions under the banner word Hinduism. These are Vaishnavism, Saktism, Saivism and Smartism. The religions grew along riverbanks because civilization thrived by the side of rivers, due to want to water. River water was essential for farming and producing food. Water, Fire, Earth, Air, and space are five sources of energies very well respected in Hinduism and in performing rituals.

SCRIPTURES

In any religion the concept is written down as guidance. Earliest literature in Hinduism is made up of four scriptures namely the four Vedas: **The Rig Veda, Sama Veda, Yajur Veda and Atharva Veda.** Rig Veda is the oldest of four Vedas. As per history, these scriptures were written by Rishis during the period 1500-800 BC. They were transmitted by oral means during Pallava—Gupta period. Many researchers are of the view that Vedas were created by decoding the secrets imbedded in cosmic vibrations by Rishis who had the capability to go into the codes through their intense meditation. In short they tapped the cosmic vibrations. How far this is true is questionable? NASA is supposed to be investigating the truths of these codes.

"Vaastu Shastram" is a science of construction and architecture based on directional alignments. Vastu had long been essentially restricted to temple architecture. It says that a Hindu temple is a representation of the cosmic world. The chakras, are the energy vortexes in the human body through which the cosmic energy penetrates into the body. Purusha means 'person' literally and refers to Universal Man. Purusha is the body of god incarnated

13

in the ground of existence, divided within the myriad forms. Vaastu Purusha is associated with the Earth and its movable and immovable basic elements of nature, such as "Pancha Boothams" namely the Earth, Water, Fire, Air and Space; just as a human being does. The Vastu purusha mandala is in some ways a development of the four pointed or cornered earth mandala having astronomical reference points.

The Vastu Purusha is visualized as lying with his face and stomach touching the ground; to suggest as if he is carrying the weight of the structure. His head is at North East and his legs are at the South West corner. The South West corner where the Vastu Purusha has his legs corresponds to the Muladhara chakra and denotes the earth principle. Just as the legs support the weight of the body, the base for the muladhara should be stable and strong. Accordingly, the South West portion of the building is the load bearing area; and should be strong enough to support heavy weights. Just as the feet are warm, the South West cell represents warmth and heat; even according to the atmospheric cycles the South West region receives comparatively more heat.

Svadhistana chakra is in the lower stomach region near the kidneys. It is related to water principle (apa). On the Vastu Purusha Mandala; it is to the South and to the West. Therefore the wet areas like bathroom etc are recommended in the south or in the west portions of the building. It is for sewerage.

The general guidelines are, the South West should be heavier and North East where gods dwell should not be so. The base should be heavy and the apex be lighter; just as in the case of a hill or a tree. The sensitive organs like brain, eyes, ears tongue are in the head; and the head should be lighter and secure. The head of the Vastu Purusha is in the North East and it should be kept free of pillars. Activities like worship, study are recommended in and towards east and adjoining directions.-North east and South East.

The sketch of the Vastu Purusah consists of 64 or 81 Squares and is called a Manadalam. Within the inner circle of the squares 12 statues of idols and in the outer circle of the square 32 statues of idols are located. The center spot is the naval position of the man and termed Brahma. Within in the inner circle of the squares the main worshiping idol such as Siva, Vishnu, Ganesh, Karthigeya (Murugan) or Sakthi (Energy) is placed. The main entrance of the temple faces in the easterly direction so that when sun rises its rays could enter the temple. A set up of the temple is the Gopuram, triangle in shape.

Vallipuram Temple Gopuram

A basic Hindu Temple consists of an inner sanctum, called the garbha griha or womb-chamber, which the image is housed, often with space for its circumambulation, an act of moving around a sacred object in a congregation hall, and possibly an antechamber and porch. The sanctum is crowned by a tower-like *shikara*. At the turn of the first millennium CE two major types of temples existed, the northern or Nagara style and the southern or

Dravida type of temple. They are distinguishable by the shape and decoration of their Gopurams.

- Nagara style: The tower is beehive shaped.
- Dravida: The tower consists of progressively smaller stories of pavilions with holes in it.

The earliest Nagara temples are in Karnataka state in India, and some very early Dravida-style temples are actually in North India. A complex style termed Vadara was once common in Karnataka which combined the two styles.

The Pallava dynasty was good in architecture and it could be inferred from Mahapalipuram structures. The Gopuram Architecture or Tamil style of architecture or Dravidian style of architecture was introduced by the Pallava dynasty. Pallava kings from Tamil Nadu were the first to evolve the Gopuram structures in temples. The Pandyas of the twelve century however popularized them to the extent that every temple in southern India began having a Gopuram. The Rajagopuram of Murudeshwara temple in Karnataka is the tallest Gopuram in the world measuring 249 feet tall and 21 floors. The second tallest Gopuram in South India is the one in Sri Ranganathaswamy Temple in Sri Rangam, Tamil Nadu. This one measures 196 feet, moving up in eleven progressive smaller tiers. The third in the list is the Sri Aandal Temple in Sirivilliputur in Tamil Nadu. It measures 192 feet tall and has 13 progressive tiers.

*   *   *

3

The Energy in a Hindu Temple

ASPECTS OF ENVIRONMENT AND ENERGY

The temple is based on combinations of symbolic figures with the purpose of making it a summary of universe and prodigious centre of energy. The cosmos is represented by mathematical formulas. Everything that exists can be reduced to proportions (Ratios) between energy elements that can be measured, whether they are planets, atoms, or matter or life

In Hinduism, the five sources of energies namely "Pancha Boothas", where Boothas refers to Energies in the world. They play an important part in rituals and in the construction of a temple for worship. The temples in India that signifies these five sources are: **Water**—Thiruvanaikovil, **Air**—Kalahasti, **Fire**—Thiruvannamalai, **Space**—Chidambaram, **Earth**—Kanchipuram or Thiruvarur.

In order to receive more solar energy from east and polar energy from north we should leave more space in our boundary on these directions. Also we should have more openings on these directions.

Vaastu "denotes in simple terms "the conditions (or) the status of energy in a land (or) building where the occupant with his complete family can live happily and lead a successful balanced growth in life. **Solar Energy: Comes** From **"Sun "**. It always flows from **East to West**. **Polar Energy: Magnetic Energy** always flows from **North Pole to South Pole.** As specified in Vedic Shastras while constructing a building we should place the "Pancha Boothas" at the appropriate locations. If we place the "Pancha Boothas" as specified by Vedic shastras, it will give harmonious positive vibrations to the occupants. If we deviate, it is a kind of dishonoring the energy which in turn will give negative vibrations to the occupants. That is why when we go into some temples we could feel the vibrations from good energy. Saadhus go to the temple to do meditation. Some devotees, after the puja, sit in a corner and meditate to achieve peace of mind.

In order to receive more solar energy from east and polar energy from north we should leave more space in our boundary on these directions. Also we should have more openings on these directions. What will happen if we do not honour these energies? It will spoil mental peace and happiness of the occupants. The occupants

and his family will not have a balanced growth in life
For example gaining only wealth with out the health (or)
Via versa is considered imbalanced growth.

VAASTU SHASTRA

Selecting site location of the Temple building is based
various criteria. Square or rectangle shape is acceptable.
The temple shape represents cosmos. Grids and
equilateral triangles are geometric shapes that prevail in
the temple. The design of the temple is a representation
of cosmos. The strict grid is a square and it is used in
performing rituals. 64 or 81 squares are termed a
mandala. The squares are located in location based on
the importance of deities. Soil testing is another aspect
of temple building. Site location is also based on people
of different castes who visit the temple for worshiping.
Vaastu Shastra prescribes desirable characteristics for
sites and buildings based on flow of energy. Many of the
rules are attributed to cosmological considerations – the
sun's path, the rotation of the earth, magnetic field, etc.,
The morning sun is considered especially beneficial and
purifying and hence the East is a treasured direction. The
body is considered a magnet with the head, the heaviest
and most important part, being considered the North pole
and the feet the South pole. Hence sleeping with one's
head in the North is believed to cause a repulsive force

with the earth's magnetic North and thus considered harmful. Bedrooms are therefore designed keeping this in mind. This is a wide spread practice in India even today.

Energy is primarily considered as emanating from the Northeast corner and many site and building characteristics are derived from this. Sites sloping down towards North or East from higher levels of South and West are considered good. Open spaces in site and openings in the building are to be more in the North and East than in the South and the West. No obstacles are to be present in the North and the East. Levels and height of buildings are to be higher in the South and West when compared to the North and East. The Southwest corner is to be the highest, followed by Southeast, then by northwest and finally by Northeast. The triangle formed by joining the Southwest, Southeast and the Northwest corner of the site is attributed to the moon and the triangle formed by joining the Northeast, Northwest and Southeast corner of the site is attributed to the sun. The former are prescribed to be heavier and higher and the latter light and lower. Sites having a longer East—West axis are considered better. The diagonal connecting southwest and Northeast is to be longer than the diagonal connecting Southeast and Northwest. An extended Northeast corner is considered beneficial.

Normally in selecting sites, the appropriate locations are near a river, pond, mountain, the place where saints were buried, and a location which is connected with a legendary story. Thiruvanamalai is a typical example of the location. Natural Energy is generated from these vital locations. The principal shrine should face the rising sun and so should have its entrance to the east. The Rays of the sun which contains cosmic solar energy enters the temple through the main entrance. The square shape is symbolic of earth, signifying the four directions which bind and define it. Indeed, in Hindu thought whatever concerns terrestrial life is governed by the number four (four castes; the four Vedas etc.). Similarly, the circle is logically the perfect metaphor for heaven since it is a perfect shape, without beginning or end, signifying timelessness and eternity, a characteristically divine attribute. Thus a mandala (and by extension the temple) is the meeting ground of heaven and earth.

- Appropriate Location of temple in a house
- Placement & direction of statue & picture's of god
- Sitting Direction of native
- Placement of earthen lamp
- Position of altar
- Prohibited raw material to use in construction in temple
- Prohibited things inside the temple
- Direction of door
- Prohibited location & rooms near to temple

- Numbers & direction of windows
- Appropriate position & direction of shelf.

The first step towards the construction of a temple is the selection of land. Even though any land may be considered suitable provided the necessary rituals are performed for its sanctification, the ancient texts nevertheless have the following to say in this matter: "The gods always play where groves, rivers, mountains and springs are near, and in towns with pleasure gardens." Not surprisingly thus, many of India do ancient surviving temples can be seen to have been built in lush valleys or groves, where the environment is thought to be particularly suitable for building a residence for the gods.

No matter where it is situated, one essential factor for the existence of a temple is water. Water is considered a purifying element in all major traditions of the world, and if not available in reality, it must be present in at least a symbolic representation in the Hindu temple. Water, the purifying, fertilizing element being present, its current, which is the river of life, can be forded into inner realization and the pilgrim can cross over to the other shore (metaphysical).

The practical preparations for building a temple are invested with great ritual significance and magical fertility symbolism. The prospective site is first inspected for the 'type,' of the soil it contains. This includes determining its color and smell. Each of these defining characteristics is divided into four categories, which are then further associated with one of the four castes:

— White Soil: Brahmin: — Red Soil: Kshatriya (warrior caste): — Yellow Soil: Vaishya — Black Soil: Shudra. Similarly for the smell and taste: Sweet: Brahmin; — Sour: Kshatriya; — Bitter: Vaishya — Astringent: Shudra

The color and taste of the soil determines the "caste" of the temple, i.e., the social group to which it will be particularly favorable. Thus the patron of the temple can choose an auspicious site specifically favorable to himself and his social environment. After these preliminary investigations, the selected ground needs to be tilled and leveled:

After the earth has been ploughed, tilled and leveled, it is ready for the drawing of the vastu-purusha mandala, the metaphysical plan of the temple. The basic plan of a Hindu temple is an expression of sacred geometry where the temple is visualized as a grand mandala. By sacred geometry we mean a science which has as its purpose the accurate laying out of the temple ground plan in relation to the cardinal directions and the heavens. Characteristically, a mandala is a sacred shape consisting of the intersection of a circle and a square.

The square shape is symbolic of earth, signifying the four directions which bind and define it. Indeed, in Hindu thought whatever concerns terrestrial life is governed by the number four (four castes; the four Vedas etc.). Similarly, the circle is logically the perfect metaphor for heaven since it is a perfect shape, without beginning or end, signifying timelessness and eternity, a characteristically divine attribute. Thus a mandala (and by extension the temple) is the meeting ground of heaven and earth.

These considerations make the actual preparation of the site and lying of the foundation doubly important. Understandably, the whole process is heavily immersed in rituals right from the selection of the site to the actual beginning of construction. Indeed, it continues to be a custom in India that whenever a building is sought to be constructed, the area on which it first comes up is ceremonially propitiated. The idea being that the extent of the earth necessary for such construction must be reclaimed from the gods and goblins that own and inhabit that area. This ritual is known as the 'pacification of the site.' There is an interesting legend behind it. It is very unfortunate that in Canada, UK, Australia, in building Hindu temples, these norms are not followed and many temples are located in ware houses. In Canada, the temples are treated as charitable institutions and hence subject to Tax benefits.

*   *   *

4

Yantras and Chakras

Shri Yantra   Swastika

The world centers on energy, the driving source. As many knows electrical, mechanical, hydro, nuclear, chemical are some of the forms of energy. Yantras refers to machines in Tamil. It conserves energy and used to generate energy. Yantras could be seen in temples and in shrines where meditation is practiced. The shape of Yantras differs. The **Sri Yantra** ("holy instrument") or **Shri Chakra** ("holy wheel") is formed by nine interlocking triangles that surround and radiate out from the central bindu point, A Yantra is a geometrical pattern made of several concentric figures (squares, circles, lotuses, triangles, point). Triangle is vital shape in construction as we have observed in Pyramids, bridges and towers. The Hindu temple has Gopuram at the entrance which is triangle in shape. When these concentric figures are gradually growing away from its center in stages, this is for human beings a symbol of the process of involution. When they are gradually growing towards its center, this is for human beings a symbol of the process of evolution.

How long can life survive in the universe? Can it evolve forever, or will the third law of Thermodynamics lead to universal heat death? Apparently there might be some ways around this fate, if intelligent life is sufficiently clever and tenacious. Essentially life has to adapt as the universe grows older, changing itself to be able to survive when the stars grow cold. If the universe is open, there will be plenty of time to work in, but energy will become very scarce. Scientists have shown that a finite amount of energy is enough to guarantee infinite survival if it is spent sufficiently slowly. On the other hand, if the universe is closed, it will re-collapse into a Big Crunch after a finite time, becoming hotter and hotter. Life has to adapt and restructure itself to these conditions, and if intelligent beings accelerate the speed of their mental processes accordingly they can even experience a subjective infinite time during the last stages of the collapse

Yantras come from the more than 2000 years old tantric tradition. A Yantra is the yogic equivalent of the Buddhist mandala. Sri Yantra is called the mother of all yantras because all other yantras are deriving from it. The Sri Yantra is a configuration of nine interlacing triangles centered around the Bindu (the central point of the Yantra), drawn by the super imposition of five downward pointing triangles, representing **Shakti** ; the female principle and four upright triangles, representing **Shiva** ; the male principle. If both Yantras are interlinked to form a pattern with six terminal points and it is termed Shivasakthi (Star of David), an important symbol of the Jews. We could also interpret it as copulation of Shakti and Shiva. The important function of Yantra is the centre point called Bindu. Energy cannot be compressed beyond this centre point of Bindu. Based on this concept, Bindu is the important point for the birth of the universe.

Brahmma is the creator of the universe and of all beings, as depicted in the Hindu cosmology. There is no person who lived with that name. It is the concept of creation of universe. When the energy was concentrated in a point called Bindu, the nuclear forces were so strong that nuclear explosion took place to over come the strong forces.

The Big Bang Theory proposes that the Universe exploded into existence about 15 billion years ago. Exact number of years is not known and is only an estimate. It started out unimaginably small, bright, hot, and dense concentration of matter, but has been expanding ever since. It now has a radius of about 15 billion light years. During the course of this expansion some of the mass of the Universe has condensed to form countless billions of stars. These stars are concentrated in galaxies, of which there are ten billion in the known Universe. These galaxies are grouped into clusters, which are themselves grouped into super clusters, separated by vast distances in empty space. The question of creation, preservation or growth and finally the decay of the universe rise. This is explained in Hinduism as Bramman for creation, Vishnu for preservation and Shiva for destruction. This goes on in cycles of million of years. The Vedas describe the cycle of evolution of life in four Yugas.

We Hindus look at time as a circle and called evolution, as things cycle around again until the soul is purified. Professor Einstein came to the same conclusion. He saw time as a curve, and space as well. This would eventually make a circle

SWASTIKA

When we speak about swastika the first thing that flashes in our mind is Nazism. We think that it is a symbol for destruction as thousands got killed in Second World War. Swastika is another Yantra used by Hindus. The Hindu swastika is different from Swastika symbol used by Adolph Hitler in Germany. It is also the symbol for Ganapathy. In Hinduism, the swastika represents the two forms of the creator god Brahma: facing right it represents the evolution of the universe, facing left it represents the involution of the universe. It is also seen as pointing in all four directions (North, East, South and West) and thus signifies stability and grounding. Its use as a sun symbol can first be seen in its representation of the god Sun. The swastika is considered extremely holy and auspicious by all Hindus, and is regularly used to decorate items related to Hindu culture. It is used in all Hindu Yantras and religious designs. Throughout the subcontinent of India, it can be seen on the sides of temples, religious scriptures, gift items, and letterheads.

The Hindu deity Ganapathy is often shown sitting on a lotus flower on a bed of swastikas. However, the swastika was also understood as "the symbol of the creating, acting life" and as "race emblem of Germanism" The word swastika is derived from Sanskrit, meaning any lucky or auspicious object, and in particular a mark made on persons and things to denote "good luck".

Swastika symbol has a lot of relevance for people in India and has been used since Vedic times and for over 3,000 years. Swastika is considered to be a mark of auspiciousness and good fortune. Though, Swastika sign is adopted by people of all religions, but it is especially popular amongst the Hindus. The swastika is considered extremely holy and auspicious by all Hindus and is regularly used to decorate items related to Hindu culture. The four limbs of the Hindu swastika is said to denote the Four Vedas, the four goals of life, the four stages of life, the four directions in space, the four seasons and the four Yugas.

The swastika symbol is one of the oldest symbols on the Earth and can be found in all religions and traditions, on all continents! The Nazi Party formally adopted the swastika in 1920. Swastika, meaning "it is well" is the symbol of auspiciousness, prosperity, and good fortune. The four limbs of the Hindu swastika denote the Four Vedas, four goals of life (denoting prosperity), four stages of life (signifying good fortune), four directions in space (symbolizing the Divine omnipresence), four seasons (symbolizing the cyclic nature of time), and four Yugas of the world-cycle (symbolizing the natural evolution of the universe).

The swastika used in Buddhist art and scripture is known as a **manji** (whirlwind), and represents Dharma, universal harmony, and the balance of opposites. It is derived from the Hindu religious swastika, but it is not identical in meaning. Archaeological evidence of swastika-shaped ornaments dates from the Neolithic period and was first found in the Indus Valley Divination. It also remains widely used in eastern religions such as Hinduism, Buddhism, Jainism, and Swastika. The word itself projects an image of hate; an image of one of the most gruesome, inhumane acts in the history of mankind. But this has not always been. The swastika was once an image of peace, fertility, and good luck. It was an image that not only traveled across cultures in Europe and Asia but has shown up in the art of Native Americans, Aztecs, and Mayans. The swastika was around 3,000 years before Hitler and the Nazi party made it an emblem of hate the swastika is notably associated with Ganesha it marks his palm. A deity who overcomes obstacles and opens the way to good fortune, Ganesh is frequently propitiated by Buddhists, as well as Hindus. In Indian festivals and other happy occasions, a swastika design is drawn on the floor of the house.

THE CHAKRAS

Chakara refer to the wheel in Tamil. When the wheel rotates it produces rotational energy. Buddhist Dhramachakra is represented with 24 spokes. The Chakras are said to be "force centers" or whirls of energy permeating, from a point in the physical body, the layers of the subtle bodies in an ever-increasing fan-shaped formation. Seven major chakras or energy centers (also understood as wheels of light) are generally believed to exist, located within the subtle body. Practitioners of Hinduism and new age spirituality believe that the chakras interact with the body's ductless endocrine glands and lymphatic system by feeding in good bio-energies and disposing of unwanted bio-energies It is typical for chakras to be depicted in one, out of two ways:

- Flower-like
- Wheel-like

Original information on Chakras come from the Upanishads, which are difficult to date because they are believed to have been passed down orally by word of mouth for approximately a thousand years before being written down for the first time between 1200-900 BC. The following seven primary chakras are commonly described:

1. Muladhara Base or Root Chakra (last bone in spinal cord)
2. Sacral Chakra (ovaries/prostate)
3. Solar Plexus Chakra (navel area)
4. Heart Chakra (heart area)
5. Throat Chakra (throat and neck area)
6. Ajna Third Eye Chakra
7. Crown Chakra (Top of the head; 'Soft spot' of a newborn)

The chakras play an important part in meditation. The energy level starts rising like the mercury in a thermometer from the Root Chakra through continuous practice and control. As it reaches each chakra the behavior of the respective chakras are felt and finally, it reaches the crown chakra. The Crown Chakra is associated with the color violet or white. We use the seventh chakra as a tool to communicate with our spiritual self. It is through this vortex that the life force is absorbed from the universe into the 6 lower chakras. This chakra is often pictured as a lotus flower opening to allow spiritual awakening in an individual. Once the energy touches this point the human body achieves the capacity to foresee and foretell things. In Hinduism, method of meditation is used to control the chakras. Ancient Rishis are evolved human-beings who had control over their chakras.

*   *   *

5

Mantras & Sound Energy

In Hinduism, Vedas claim that "Speech is the essence of humanity". All what humanity thinks and ultimately becomes is determined by the expression of ideas and actions through speech and its derivative, writing. In Vedic practices, and in most Buddhist techniques, mantra is viewed as a necessity for spiritual advancement and high attainment. The word Mantra is a Sanskrit word hence a literal translation would be "a mind tool". Mantras are interpreted to be effective as sound (vibration), to the effect that great emphasis is put on correct pronunciation and tone. Vibration contains energy, and is based on frequency of vibration of the sound waves. The tone soothes the mind and helps in meditation.

Ultra-sound is used in medical treatment and exploration. Combination of low frequencies and low power represent a sweet spot where the sound readily penetrates the skull and affects brain cells. Mantras generate sound wave that can heal people who suffer from brain disorders. A pregnant woman who chants mantras daily helps the fetus in the womb to grow healthily.

Mantras originated in the Vedic tradition of India and later became an essential part of Hindu tradition and a customary practice within Buddhism, Sikhism & Jainism. The syllable AUM, constituting a mantra in itself, represents Brahamman. The scientist believes that AUM is the sound that was created with the formation of Universe as a result of Big bang. The vibration filled the whole universe. The most basic mantra is Aum, which in Hinduism is known as the "pranava mantra," the source of all mantras. In Christianity it is called AMEN and in Islam it spelt as AMIN. All elements and energies in the Cosmos can be influenced and guided by Mantras. There are three types of Mantras: In Buddhism chanting Pirith is a repetition of mantras to drive away bad energy.

- Prayer is a way of communing with God.
- Guru mantra. The Guru Mantra represents the essence of prayer, and anchors us in God, the Aatma and the Supreme Self. It is the first initiation given by the Master to the disciple on the spiritual path.
- Bija mantra represents the essence of the Guru Mantra. It is the vibration and the "call" of the

soul. Its effects develop more readily in deep meditation. As it works at the astral level it guides and influences the course of our destiny.

Continuous practice of mantras purify the Consciousness and the mind, and removes the Karmas in much the same way as how constantly walking over weeds crushes them It involves repetition of a mantra over and over again, repeatedly, usually in cycles of auspicious numbers (in multiples of three), the most popular being 108.

SIGNIFICANCE OF 108.

108 is a popular number in religions and mainly Hinduism in the same way as 786 is in Islam. Many explanations are given for selecting this number 108. It could have been otherwise, but it so happens that the distance between the earth and the sun equals about 108 (actually 107-odd) times the sun's diameter. Likewise, the distance between the earth and the moon equals about 108 (actually 109-odd) times the moon's diameter. That sun and moon look equally big in the earthly sky is the immediate result of their having the same ratio between distance and diameter. Moreover, the sun's diameter approximately equals 108 times the earth's diameter.

There is another scientific explanation for 108 related to human body. The chakras are also the intersections of energy lines, and there are said to be a total of 108 energy lines converging to form the heart chakra. One of them, leads to the crown chakra, and is said to be the path to Self-Realization. In astrology, there are 12 houses and 9 planets. 12 x 9 = 108. Other religions too give prominence for this number. In many religions a Japa (chanting) Chain contains 108 beads for counting the mantra when recited. In Chinese astrology, the Tao philosophy holds that there are 108 sacred stars. In Islam, the number 108 is used to refer to God. In Hindu temples 108 flames are shown when Puja is done for deities. The number 108 is most sacred in Hindu-Buddhist civilization.

SANSKRIT LANGUAGE & MANTRA.

Mantras are energy based sounds. Saying any word produces an actual physical vibration. During meditation one way of concentrating is to repeat the word "Ohm Namasivaya". Over time, if we know what the effect of that vibration is, then the word may come to have meaning associated with the effect of saying that vibration or word. This is one level of energy basis for words.

The main political issue in Tamil nadu is the use of Sanskrit while doing Pujas in Temples. The general public is of the opinion that Brahmin caste is in overall control of Sanskrit language and claim that they are the only race which is eligible to chant mantras. The main reason given is purity in the way of lifestyle and the art of chanting mantras is passed from generation to generation. Another explanation is that Brahmins fear that their profession and income will be lost if chanting mantras is translated into Tamil. The Suseendram temple in Nagarkovil carries a Tamil board and insists that Pujas should be performed in Tamil. The same notice appears in many temples including Chithambaram. The belief is that when mantras are chanted in Sanskrit language, the phonetic vibration generates an effective impact on the human body. Even communication in Iranian language is soft and pleasant to hear. However, understanding the text of chanting is vital for devotees.

Sound & Light

Sound and Light are energy waves, travel at different speeds but actions are different. This is exhibited in lightning and sound of thunder and explained in Hinduism as two different gods with different power. For the growth of the human brain, both energies are vital. Recently there was a news item about a popular south Indian music composer Illayarajah from Tamil Nadu who composed Music for Thiruvasagam. A

German couple found that their baby in the womb of the mother did not show any movements. When the baby's fetus was exposed to the Thiruvasagam music of Illayarajah, it showed signs of movements. In the course of time, due to constant exposure to the music, the baby was normal at delivery. Babies when repeatedly exposed to the sound of Musical instruments in the course of time, become great musicians. Both energy waves take important places in Hinduism. Sound waves are vital for mantras, and light waves are vital for showing flames to statues.

In Hindu idols, Damarum is held by Shiva, flute by lord Krishna, Veena by Goddess Saraswathy, Miruthangam by Nandhi. Damarum is a small hourglass shaped drum, and is particularly associated with Shiva in his aspect as the Nadaraja, performing the cosmic dance of tandava. The sound of damaru represents the primeval sound and the rhythm from which, according to cosmology, the universe emerges and in which it dissolves into, before re-emerging again. The damaru is known as a power drum, and when played, it is believed to generate spiritual energy. The blowing of the conch symbolizes the primordial creative voice and Indian mysticism links it to the sacred sound AUM, which is said to be the breath of Vishnu, pervading all space. Try holding a conch shell to your ear, the sound of the ocean humming gently can be heard. It is actually the natural vibration or cosmic energy of the earth that gets magnified on entering the conch shell. These unique whirls are directed clockwise in perfect synchronization with universal harmony. That is why a conch shell is blown during sacred rites to get rid of negative energy. The vibrations from these conch shells can dispel evil forces from the earth and also clear environmental pollution including healing the hole in the ozone layer which causes global warming!"

The warriors of ancient India blew conch shells to announce battle, as is described in the beginning of the war of Kurukshetra, in the famous Hindu epic Mahabharata. Conch shell is blown in rituals, especially when dead bodies are carried to the funeral pyre. Instruments such as Flute, Drums, Miruthangam, Gadam, Veena, Violin, Tabla, are some instruments created from the sources of nature. In Hinduism this establishes the link between natures from where those products had their origin. The sounds from these instruments are used in Hindu rituals. Nadaswaram and Melam are two popular instruments, used in Tamil nadu Hindu temples.

Music plays an important part in Hinduism specially in singing bajans and in festivals. Nadaswaram and Melam (drum) are prominent instruments in Tamil nadu, Sri Lankan and Malaysian Hindu temples. It has become a tradition to use these instruments along with Barthanatyam dance. In the past, there were temple dancers dedicated to god, for performing dance in temples and they were called "Devadasi" (Servants of god). This tradition has gradually disappeared as Devadasi's were misused by rich people of the village.

Mantras create thought-energy waves.

Mantras start a powerful vibration which corresponds to both a specific spiritual energy frequency and a state of consciousness in seed form. Over time, the mantra process begins to override all of the other smaller vibrations, which eventually become absorbed by the mantra. After a length of time which varies from individual to individual, the great wave of the mantra stills all other vibrations. Ultimately, the mantra produces a state where the organism vibrates at the rate completely in tune with the energy and spiritual state represented by and contained within the mantra. Within the human body vibration continues

And the heart vibrates to generate energy.

At this point, a change of state occurs in the organism. The organism becomes subtly different. Just as a laser is light which is coherent in a new way, the person who becomes one with the state produced by the mantra is also coherent in a way which did not exist prior to the conscious undertaking of repetition of the mantra.

MANTRA ENERGIZES PRANA.

"Prana" is a Sanskrit term for a form of life energy which can be transferred from individual to individual. Prana may or may not produce an instant dramatic effect upon transfer. There can be heat or coolness as a result of the transfer.

Some healers operate through transfer of prana. A massage therapist can transfer prana with beneficial effect. Even self-healing can be accomplished by concentrating prana in certain organs, the result of which can be a clearing of the difficulty or condition. For instance, by saying a certain mantra while visualizing an internal organ bathed in light, the specific power of the mantra can become concentrated there with great beneficial effect.

DIFFERENT FORMS OF HINDU MANTRAS:

Along with Aum Namasivaya, Gayatri Mantra, *Vishnu sahasranāma*, Ganapthy mantra are some of the many mantras practiced in Hinduism. Each has a purpose. The sacred and most important Gayatri mantra consisting of 24 syllables is taken from a hymn of the Rig-Veda. Its recitation is always preceded by Om and the formula *bhūr bhuvaḥ svaḥ*, the "great mystical phrase". The manifestation of the omnipresent power of Gayatri in the cosmic expansion of eternal sound was discovered by Maharshi Vishwamitra. The Vishnu *sahasranāma* (literally: "the thousand names of Vishnu) is a list of 1,000 names for Vishnu, in the epic Mahabharata, the names were handed down to Yudhisthira by the famous warrior Bhishma who was on his death bed at the battle of Kurushestra. Bhisma answers by stating that mankind will be free from all sorrows by chanting the *Vishnu sahasranāma'*

*   *   *

6

Nature & Hinduism

"Nature" refers to the phenomena of the physical world, and also to life in general. It ranges in scale from the subatomic to the cosmic. Earth is the only planet presently known to support life, and as such, its natural features are the subject of many fields of scientific research. Earth is estimated to have been formed 4.55 billion years ago from the solar nebula along with the Sun and other planets.

Nature and Hinduism are so entwined that it is quite impossible to think about one without the other. The need for an ecological balance is stressed in the Vedas and Upanishads and this message is repeated in the Ramayana, Mahabharata, Gita, and Puranas and in the messages of Hindu saints. Symbolism in Hinduism centers on nature. Mother Nature is worshipped in Hindu religion. But for majority of Hindus, worship is confined to temples and homes and thus they are equal contributors to global warming, pollution and emissions.

Earth is called "Boomadevi" and is respected highly in Hinduism. In Ramayana Sita, the wife of Rama was found from the earth so says the legendary story.

The main components of nature are animals, birds, insects, plants, forests, herbs, mountains, rivers, streams and ponds. Herbs are used in rituals to purify the air. "Thulasi" plant is treated as holy plant and worshiped from home. They all contain energy and are useful for mankind. Man at times taps energy from them for their livelihood. The energies of animals such as Bulls, Horses, Elephants are used in war and to do hard work. Firewood provides Thermal energy and water Hydro energy. Sun rays provide solar energy. The older religions saw (divine) spirit in every tree, river, animal and bird. That is why in Hinduism we still notice devotees worshipping Snake, Peacock, cow, monkey (Hanuman) and stones. Rig Veda says one should not destroy trees and plants and they should be treated as mothers and Goddesses. Sacred grass should be protected from man's exploitation. No religion, perhaps, lays as much emphasis on environmental ethics as does Hinduism. It believes in ecological responsibility and says like Native Americans that the Earth is our mother. It champions protection of animals, which it considers also have souls, and promotes vegetarianism. It has a strong tradition of non-violence or ahimsa. It believes that God is present in all nature, in all creatures, and in every human being regardless of their faith or lack of it.

Each temple has a special tree. Vilvam, Marutham, Vembu, Arasu, Tulasi, Banyan are some of the many trees worshiped by Hindus. In Kancheepuram, a very old mango tree called Amba in the temple is considered sacred. Amba refers to Ambal. Each tree has its own form of energy, and herbal value. Every Hindu deity is associated with a bird or an animal. During festivals the deities are mounted on a statue of an animal or bird. Nadarajar on Nanthi, Murugan on Peacock, Ganapathy on mouse, Vishnu on Garuda, Kali on lion, and Saturn on crow and Vairavar on dog are considered as their respective vehicles. Each of these has a philosophical explanation for its association and also signifies the respect for nature. Even special grass is used in rituals. Sages often sit on Kusha grass mats when they do their meditation. Trees possess energy. People do meditation under a Tree. Buddha attained Nirvana under a Bo Tree. Ramana Mahrishi meditated in the Virupaksha Cave. The cave is situated on Arunachala Mountain about 700 feet above the town of Thirumvannamalai. Ramana Maharshi meditated for 17 years in this cave. Devotees do "Girivalam"; walking about 17 Km around the Thirivannamalai Mountain to get the feeling of vibration of energy generated from the mountain and the breathing of unpolluted air from nature. Hindus first perceived God's presence around them through nature. The natural forces that governed their daily lives were considered as manifestations of an Almighty Creator they called the Brahamman.

Ancient Hindus felt Brahman's presence in everything around them. Since these divine forces sustained all living creatures and organic things on this earth, to please God, they felt they must live in harmony with His creation including earth, rivers, forests, sun, air, and mountains. This belief spawned many rituals that are still followed by traditional Hindus in India. For example, before the foundation of a building is laid, a priest is invited to perform the Bhoomi Pooja in order to worship and appease mother earth and seek forgiveness for violating her. Certain plants, tries and rivers were considered sacred, and worshipped in festivals. In a traditional Hindu family, to insult or abuse nature is considered a sacrilegious act. A Hindu mother would severely scold her child for acts like ripping the limb of a plant or urinating or spitting on a tree or in any body of water.

This Hindu prayer called Shanti path recited to conclude every Hindu ceremony, reflect the Hindus' connectedness with nature: "There is peace in heavenly region; there is peace in the environment; the water is cooling; herbs are healing; the plants are peace-giving; there is harmony in the celestial objects and perfection in knowledge; everything in the universe is peaceful; peace pervades everywhere. May that peace be there every where.

Modern Hindus have forgotten their ancestors' view on ecology, and have acquired the Western exploitative attitude towards nature. Lush forests have been denuded, rivers, including the sacred river the Ganges, have become polluted with industrial wastes. Delhi has become one of the most polluted cities in the world. Many beautiful birds and animals have become extinct. This devastation is taking place in the name of progress.

The sacred trees or temple trees along with the sacred groves and sacred tanks are the three most important ecological traditions of Tamilnadu and have played a significant role in the protecting and preserving the environment. Each sacred tree is associated with a deity and a temple. Sacred trees are revered and worshipped by the devotees with specific taboos and customs. The 60 Temple trees surveyed and recorded were all found to have medicinal and mythological stories. In Hinduism, devotees go around the statue of a snake to be blessed with a child. Snakes are worshiped with great respect and Temples are there for snakes in Lanka and Tamil Nadu. The ancient race called Nagas were worshippers of snake. Legendary stories are written about the temples of snakes to make people believe in them. Many plants such as Thulasi are considered to be holy. Plants are often associated with many myths and folklore. The plants are associated and identified with Gods, planets, months, etc. Certain plants are used for protection against witchcraft and the evil eye. Some plants bring luck and are offered in the temples and others play an important part in other religious rites. The trees featured in mythology are the Banyan and the Papal trees in Hinduism, and the modern tradition of the Christmas tree is from Germanic mythology.

Different trees have different significance in Hinduism. Here are some of them. Legendary stories are built around the trees to establish the relationship with different idol worship.

Ashoka Tree — Ashoka is one of the most legendary and sacred trees of India. Ashoka is a Sanskrit word meaning without grief or that which gives no grief. Of course, the tree has many other names in local languages as well. One such name means the tree of love blossoms. The tree is a symbol of love. King Asoka fought a war in Kalinga (Orissa state) in India, killed thousands of people, later realized his mistake and converted himself as Buddhist went in search of peace. His sister Sangamitta introduced Buddhism in Sri Lanka. Its beautiful, delicately perfumed flowers are used in temple decoration. Lord Buddha was born under the Ashoka tree, so it is planted in Buddhist monasteries.

Banyan Tree—Like Papal Tree, the Banyan Tree also symbolizes the Trimurti-Lord Vishnu, Lord Shiva and Lord Brahma. The tree also symbolizes life and fertility in many Hindu cultures. That is the reason, why the banyan tree is worshiped by those who are childless and also that this tree should never be cut. The tree can grow into a giant tree covering several hectares. The Great Banyan in the Indian Botanic Garden, Howrah, is considered to be the largest tree in the world. Banyan trees are sacred in South Asia, particularly to Hindus and Buddhists. The tree features in many myths. The tree represents eternal life because it supports its expanding canopy by growing special roots from its branches. In Hinduism the banyan tree represents immortality. In the legendary story tale of Satyavan and Savitri, Satyavan lost his life beneath the branches of a banyan. Savitri courageously entered into a debate with Yama, the God of Death, and won his life back. The Hindus believe that married women visit a banyan and pray for the long life of their husbands. The tree is associated with the life of the 15th century saint Kabir. A giant tree is said to have sprung from a twig he had chewed. People of all religions use its great leafy canopy to meditate or rest.

Bael Tree—In India, Bael tree is considered to be very sacred because it is associated with Lord Shiva. It is said that Lord Shiva is pleased by offerings of leaves from the Bael Tree, also known as bilva or bel tree. Thus, the Brahmanas worshiped Lord Shiva by for a period of one fortnight by offering bel leaves and that way satisfied Lord Shiva greatly. The fruit, flowers and leaves of the tree are all sacred to Shiva. Planting these trees around home or temple is sanctifying and is equivalent to worshiping a Linga with bilva leaves and water. The trifoliate leaf or tripatra of the bael tree is believed to symbolize the three functions of the Lord-the creation, preservation and destruction as well as his three eyes. The offering of the leaves is a compulsory ritual while worshipping Lord Shiva all over India. The Beal tree is also sacred to the Jains.

Bamboo Tree—The common names of Lord Krishna-Venugopal, Bansilal, Murali and Muralidhar reflect his association with Bansuri or Venu, his constant companion. Bansuri is actually a flute made of bamboo. That is the reason, bamboo is revered in India because it is associated with Lord Krishna. It is said that bamboo shoot should not be harvested by a Brahmin, as it is compared to a killing child of the family. Similarly Brahmins should not plant bamboo or a banana, they usually hire a people of other caste to do so. But on the other hand, on all Brahmin wedding, bamboo and a banana are mandatory, and the corpse is always carried on a bamboo stretcher.

Banana Tree — Though banana is not a tree but it is considered a tree because of its structure and size. It is a very sacred tree and all parts of the tree are used for some purpose or the other. For example, the trunk of banana is used to erect welcoming visitors at the gates. The leaves are used to make the ceremonial pavilion. In some pooja, the leaves are used to serve "prashad". Just as leaves of bel tree are customarily offered to Lord Siva, it is believed that offering of the leaves of banana pleases Lord Ganesha. Banana as a fruit is offered to Lord Vishnu and Lakshmi.

Coconut Tree: — Breaking a coconut in ritual signifies breaking of egoism in the soul. The coconut) which is used in the making of a Purna-Kumbha (kalash) is also an independent object of worship. A coconut — is the fruit of God, alone is also used to symbolize 'God' while worshipping any deity. The three eyes of the coconut represent the three eyes of Shiva. In India one of the most common offerings in a temple is a coconut. It is also offered on occasions like weddings, festivals, the use of a new vehicle, bridge, house etc. It is offered in the sacrificial fire whilst performing Shanthi at homa. The coconut is broken and placed before the Lord. It is later distributed as prasaada.

The structure of the coconut also has been given a deep spiritual significance. As defined in the Vedanta (the ultimate book of knowledge) man is made up of the **Gross Body** (physical body), **Subtle Body** (mind – that is relating to world), **Causal Body** (a higher state of mind) and the Aatman (soul/true self). The smooth outer skin of the coconut represents man's Gross Body. Within the Gross body is the subtle body of mind, this is represented by the matted coir of the coconut, indicating the desires and attachments of man with the outer world. The hard shell represents the Causal Body and the white inside the Kernel represents the Self. When the coconut is cut open, the white colour indicates the purity of the soul.

Lotus – The Lotus is always considered as an evocative symbol of beauty, purity and divinity and a highly revered flower by all Hindus. The flowers have been sacred in Asia and the Middle East for over 5000 years and frequently occur in Hindu and Buddhist art and literature. In Hinduism many of the deities are pictured sitting upon a lotus or holding a lotus flower. The lotus represents the manifestation of God. The pure white lotus flower is the only plant to fruit and flower simultaneously. Saraswathi Goddess of learning resides in the white lotus. The red lotus flower is a symbol of Goddess Laxmi. One of the incarnations of the Mother-Goddess or Devi and wife of the Hindu god Vishnu, Laxmi is the goddess of fortune and prosperity as well as the epitome of feminine beauty. According to Hindu mythology she was born radiant and fully grown from the churning of the sea. Lakshmi is always portrayed as sitting on a lotus flower which is her traditional symbol. That is why this flower is held in high esteem. The Lotus flower has also symbolized spiritual enlightenment. It is said that the Lotus in Eastern Culture has a similar symbolism to the Rose in Christianity. Buddhists too respect the Lotus flower

Thulasi — is always associated with purity, is highly revered and is used for all religious purposes among the Hindus. It is considered very auspicious to have a Thulasi plant in the front courtyard of many Hindu households. The smell of the tree prevents snakes from entering the house. Thulasi beads can always be seen around the necks of serious yogis and mystics in India, worn to purify the mind, emotions and body. Dispelling the unwanted influences of others, gross and subtle, is one of the many benefits bestowed by Thulasi plant and hence it is worshipped by all. Thulasi plants are also valued in Ayurveda, where they are considered an integral part of that sophisticated healing system. In practically every temple in India, no puja can be started without few Thulasi leaves. There is always a special place reserved for this sacred plant. The qualities and amazing powers of this plant are found throughout the oldest writings on Earth, the Sanskrit Vedas of ancient

India, where it is stated that simply touching the wood is purifying at many levels. Thulasi plant is most loved by Lord Vishnu and Vrinda Devi, the Goddess ruling Tulsi is known as the personification of bhakti or devotion to the Supreme Being. These are some of the many plants in nature which have significance Hinduism. Many of them are herbal and used as medicine by people.

NATIVE AMERICAN INDIANS AND NATURE.

The environment hugely affected the Native American Indians in many different ways. This is because of the way in which the Indians used the environment and the surrounding land. The Indians were very close to nature, and so that meant that any changes in nature would be changes in the Indians. They respect the trees. They discourage the destruction of forests and land. The Native American culture includes famous dances to respect nature. This is similar to the dances in India for specific Hindu gods with appropriate music. Some of the dances by the American Indians are for Deer, Rain, Buffalo, Dog Dance, Green Corn etc, Most of these dances were specific to the culture of individual tribes.

The American Indians view the white man's attitude to nature as the polar opposite of the Indian. The white man seemed hell-bent on destroying not just the Indians, but the whole natural order, felling forests, clearing land, killing animals for sport. Their main aim was to make money. Pines are symbolically and ceremonially important trees to many Native American people, but their meaning varies from tribe to tribe. The pine tree is a symbol of longevity to the Algonquian tribes of the northeast, The Iroquois tribes saw the pine tree as a symbol of peace, and burned pine wood as an incense to pacify ghosts and banish nightmares. Animals are respected as equal in rights to humans. Religious beliefs varied between tribes, but there was a widespread belief in a Great Spirit who created the earth, and who pervaded everything.

According to Iroquois legend, the Great Spirit had told them that the animals and the things of the forest were their helpers. They knew they needed trees and plants and animals to live. But they were still sorry when they had to take a life for their existence.

They were very careful to take only what they absolutely needed. To the Iroquois and other Woodland Indians, it would have been an insult to kill something and then waste it. A tree was living, and therefore sacred. If you were going to chop down a tree, every part of it had to be helpful. This shows how American Indians respect the Nature

* * *

7

The Solar System & Hinduism

Hinduism respects the elements of solar system because it is believed that life of humans is influenced by the Solar system. Navagraha, worshiping of nine planets, is a common ritual in Hinduism. Pujas are held for Saturn and Jupiter for those who are under the bad influence of those planets. This is based on the belief by Hindus that planets influence their life on this earth and hence the horoscope is cast as a soon as child is born. The horoscope is used to predict the destiny, health, marriage, profession, wealth and death of the man. Sun and Moon are considered as planets in Hinduism. Ragu and Kethu, the nodal points of intersection of the two planes of orbits of the sun and moon too are considered as planets. These nodal points differ by 180 degrees. Hence so are the positions of the Ragu and Kethu in the horoscope. The time of birth, longitude and latitude of the place of birth and the time of sun rise on the day of birth are taken as the base in casting the horoscope. The

Tamil and Sinhala New Year start between 14th and 15th of April each year when sun enters the house of Capricorn. There are 12 houses each 30 degrees each and the sun resides approximately one month in each house. There is a continuous cycle of sixty years and sixty names are given which depict the behavior of the year. Hindus and Buddhists in Sri Lanka have many things in common on New Year day. Wearing a new dress, Exchanging money, Starting a new business, Starting a relationship, visiting a Temple or Vihara and more cultural activities have significance on this day.

According to Hindu mythology and Vedic cosmology the universe is cyclically created and destroyed. The life span of Lord Brahma, the creator, is 100 'Brahma-Years'. One day in the life of Brahma is called a Kalpa or 4.32 billion years. We are currently believed to be in the 51st year of the present Brahma's life and so about 158.7 trillion years have elapsed since the birth of Brahma. After Brahma's "death", it is necessary that another 100 Brahma years pass until he is reborn and the whole creation begins anew. Brahamma is not a living being but only a concept. This process is repeated again and again, forever. Both the Rig-Veda and Brahmanda Purana describe a Universe that is cyclical or oscillating and infinite in time. The universe is described as a cosmic egg that moves in cycles between expansion and total collapse. It expanded from a concentrated form of energy at a point called a Bindu. The universe, as a living entity, is bound to the perpetual cycle of birth, death and rebirth. The theory of reincarnation originated from this concept.

The cosmic egg is an ancient concept resurrected by modern science in the 1930s and explored by theoreticians during the following two decades. The idea comes from a perceived need to reconcile Edwin Hubble's observation of an expanding universe which is also predicted by Einstein's equations of general relativity. Current cosmological models maintain that 13.7 billion years ago, the entire mass of the universe was compressed into a singularity, from which it expanded to its current state (the Big Bang), the so-called cosmic egg.

Aryabhata was a Hindu mathematical astronomer born in India around 475 AD. By the age of 23 he had already published his most significant work named as **Aryabhatiya.** Aryabhata was a pioneer in the field of mathematics and astronomy. Most of his works were lost. His major work **Aryabhatiya** was in fact named by his disciples. The mathematical part of the **Aryabhatiya** covers arithmetic, algebra, plane and spherical trigonometry, continued fractions, quadratic equations, sums of power series and a table of Sine. Hence the greatest contribution of **Aryabhatiya** was the decimal place value notation without which mathematics, science and commerce would be impossible. Aryabhata also calculated the sidereal rotation of Earth (the rotation of the earth referenced the fixed stars) as 23 hours 56 minutes and 4.1 seconds and the modern value is 23 Hrs: 56Minutes :4.091 seconds. How close are two independent computations?

The Sun God is worshiped as a deity or an aspect of it, usually by its perceived power and strength. People have worshiped these for all of recorded history. Hence, many beliefs have formed around this worship, such as the "missing sun" found in many cultures. Many cultures have worshiped the sun or a physical representation of the sun throughout history. According to the Egyptian account of creation, only the ocean existed at first. Then Ra, the sun, (Called Ravi in Tamil) came out of an egg (a flower, in some versions) that appeared on the surface of the water. The only important God who was worshiped with consistency was Ra, chief of cosmic deities, from whom early Egyptian kings claimed descent. Beginning with the Middle Kingdom (2134-1668 BC), Ra worship acquired the status of a state religion. The hymns tell of Surya's chariot being drawn across the sky by seven bay mares. Seven seems to be an important number in many religions. Seven may be significant because there are seven visible celestial bodies that wander across the sky, the Sun, Moon, and the five planets visible to the naked eye, Mercury, Venus, Mars, Jupiter and Saturn. Because they are all wanderers we can call them planets, even though today we normally do not think of the Sun and Moon as planets. The Sun Temple, built in the thirteenth century, in Konark Orissa, was conceived as a gigantic chariot of the Sun God, with twelve pairs of exquisitely ornamented wheels pulled by seven pairs of horses. It was constructed from oxidized and weathered ferruginous sandstone by King Narasimha deva (1238-1250 CE) of the eastern Ganga Dynasty. Some scientists say that the seven horses signify the seven colours in spectrum formed from the Sun's rays. Isaac Newton invented seven colors in the white light during 18th century long after the temple was built hence many questions are raised whether he borrowed the concept from the chariot of the Sun God.

Sun worship in India dates back to ancient times. Sun Worship is a ritual followed by thousands of devotees of Hinduism. Most Hindus start their day by worshipping the sun God. It is believed that worshipping this God gives energy and good health, which in turn leads to wealth / money and prosperity. References to sun worship are found in the Vedas and Puranas. All living beings on the face of earth get their life force only due to the rays of sun. Hindus therefore worship Sun as the life giver of the entire universe and witness of all actions. In the Hindu calendar has the first day of the week is named after the sun God. In legends the Sun God is portrayed as seated on a chariot drawn by seven horses.

The Sun is the lord of the Zodiac Sign Leo. The sun stays one month in each Zodiac and takes 365 days or 1 year to complete an orbit of the 12 signs. Surya exalts in the sign of Aries and falls in the sign of Libra. The Sun is beneficial for those born under the zodiac signs of Aries, Leo, and Sagittarius. According to Indian Astrology a well-located Sun in the horoscope indicates intelligence, good health, confidence, leadership qualities, courage, strength, independence, fame, success, power, vitality and straight-forwardness in an individual. But an ill-placed Sun could mean ill health, lack of endurance, low vitality, fear and dependency. However an overly strong or poor placement of the Sun may bring in some negative qualities in people. Sun Worship is very helpful for those who face problems, hurdles and misfortune in their lives. It is also said to be helpful in curing diseases like eye problems, leprosy, heart problems, nervous disorders, asthma etc. To get gain benefits of the Sun one can fast on Sundays and take salt free food.

Unfortunately, the term Graha was linked to the term "planet" of our solar system as five members of Navagraha (the nine grahas) happen to be planets; but the Surya (sun), Chandra (moon), Rahu, ascending lunar node and Ketu, descending lunar node are not "planets" according to modern astronomy. This misconception is sometimes used as arguments against the validity of astrology. There are deities for Rahu and Kethu. Rahu is represented by the head of the snake and Kethu the tail. This indicates a difference of 180 degrees in the two nodes.

In Tamilnadu, around Kumbakonam temples are located for all planets. The temple for sun is at Suriyanar, 15 km from Kumbakonam. Famous temple for Saturn is at Thirunallaru. Jupiter has a temple in Alangudi. Temple for Mars is at Vaideeswaran. Moon too has a temple in Thingaloor. Moon influences the mind of the humans and as such Hindus believe that if the Moon ill placed in the horoscope, the person can become a lunatic or commit suicide. The Moon, with its emotional sensitivity, has traditionally been viewed as feminine. The Sun, with its charisma and force, has been seen as masculine.

The moon is the celestial body which is most visible in the nightly sky. The moon dominates the night sky and can be seen far more clearly than any other planet or star. The phases of the moon are one of humankind's best and most ancient means of measuring time. "Moon," "menses," and "month" all share the same root, meaning to measure. The most visible symbol of feminine energy in the solar system is the Moon. Because it reflects the light from the sun, the pale orbit in the night sky has come to represent a woman's reflective nature, her internalized response to the world.

The coincidence of the menstrual cycle with that of the moon is a physical actuality structuring human life and a curiosity that has been observed with wonder. It is in fact likely that the fundamental notion of life-structuring relationship between the heavenly world and that of man was derived from this realization, both in experience and in thought, of the force of the lunar cycle.

The sun is the chief of all Navagrahas, the 9 planet-Gods and is represented by the number one. The gemstone and metal associated with this planet is gold and Ruby. The sun is especially worshiped on **"Makara Sankaranthi"** day which falls in the month of January. There are several temples dedicated to the Sun, some of them are the Sun Temple at Konark, Dakshinaarka Temple in Gaya, Suryanar Kovil in Tamilnadu and Suryanarayana Temple at Arasavilli. The Gayatri Mantra, one of the most sacred of Hindu Mantras is dedicated to the Sun. Apart from this many Shiva temples also have shrines dedicated to the Sun God. This gives us a clue as to the link between the sun and the cosmic dance of Lord Nadarjah.

Hindu astrology involves mathematics in calculating Sun-rise time and movement of the Planets and Sun set. It also predicts the exact date and time a lunar or total solar or annular eclipse will occur and the places in the world it could be seen 100%. This amazing calculation coincides with recent scientific calculations proving the link between Hinduism and science. Hinduism and Astrology have links with the solar system through human lives. Astrological predictions based on horoscopes may not always come true, but it is the belief in astrology, that plays an important part in the outcome. Matching of horoscopes between the boy and the girl has become a culture among the Hindus, and the present generation calls it matching of chemistry.

Hinduism has traditionally held that there are certain times and days that are better to hold or to begin important events, such as marriage, particular religious rituals, even business ventures.

*   *   *

8

Relativity and Time Dilation

Many students are aware of the three dimensions in solid state mathematics represented by X, Y, Z directions. Space is measurable in these three directions which are at right angled to each other. The additional concept of Time is considered as the fourth dimension and is needed for imagination. It is hard to try to directly picture the fourth dimension in our minds. It is interrelated with all 3 axis and as such we cannot show it as an axis right angled to x, y, z, as time affects the length in all three directions. The velocity is the distance traveled in a particular direction, divided by time taken to travel. Time is not a vector but a scalar quantity. Time existed from the time space existed. Time is eternal and flows. It is related to birth, life and death. In the Vedas we refer to Manuvantras and Kalpas and in Astronomical science vast distance is referred by light year that is the distance travelled by light in one year.

A Kalpa in Hinduism is 8.64 trillium years. In Hinduism Time is important in Human life and in rituals. Hindu almanacs is based on planetary movement, specially the Sun, Moon and Time, The basic number is 432,000 years, the age of Kali **Yuga**, and so Dwa**para** Yuga which is twice that number, **Treta** Yuga is 3 times that number and **Satya Yuga** is four times that number. One rotation of these four Yugas is called a Yuga cycle which is a total of 4,320,000 years.

The highest speed attainable is the velocity of light "c" which is about 300,000 kilometers per second. According to Albert Einstein's special theory of relativity, c is an important constant connecting space and time in the unified structure of space-time. As such, it defines the conversion between mass (m) and energy (E) by the famous mass energy equation $E=mc^2$ and is an upper bound on the speed at which matter and information can travel. At a particular speed called velocity of light "c" the associated Energy converts mass into wave nature. This concept is nothing new to Hinduism. Rishis experienced this dual nature to communicate with the cosmos and unite the hidden secrets into the Vedas.

The transition from the third dimension into the fourth comes when our subconscious has released itself from opposing forces sufficiently, to recognize that awareness travels in the mind and to identify the self with awareness, instead of with states of emotion through which the intellect passes. The fourth dimension then is the sub superconscious faculty of man. It is a beautiful place to be, and you can be there always by feeling the power of your spine. The minute you feel that radiant energy in the spine you are disconnected from the third dimension and start to soar into the fourth. This is how the Rishis enjoyed their experiences during the Vedic period. Hindu Mythology has concept of Space travel—Narada and other Rishis, and all Gods can travel to any place in the cosmos according to legendary stories in Hindi mythology. Is Time Travel also a concept of Hindu Mythology? Mass, Length and Time change with velocity. The change called dilation is noticeable only when the speed approaches closer to the velocity of light. As it touches the velocity of light, mass which is the quantity of matter present, becomes bigger and bigger and tends to infinity so is the length. This transformation may be called wave form and termed dual nature of mass. The scientific fiction story "Time Machine" is based on Relativity. So the Rishis had the capacity to live in different time frames before and after the existing period to perceive things.

The cosmos is everything that exists. The universe is a subset of the cosmos and contains all of the galaxies and other stuff that has mass, including areas that have not yet been seen. The so-called Big Bang theory is the current favored hypothesis of the formation of the universe according to astronomy. This asserts that some 12-15 billion years ago there was a sudden expansion and explosion of all matter and energy out of an original point (Bindu) – out of literally nothing – and that not only space but even time began at this event. (So we cannot speak of an explosion in space – because there was no space before, or no time at which this could be measured – space and time being properties of the universe rather than something outside of it). Earlier versions of the Big Bang theory had the universe originating from a singularity (a point of zero volume and infinite density, where the laws of physics have no meaning).

In nature the matter should first exist in a place and then change in size with time and finally come to an end. In brief we call it birth, growth and death and defined in Hinduism as the functions of Brahma, Vishnu and Siva respectively. Cosmos functions on a cyclic basis.

Time dilation – is a great concept indeed. Albert Einstein, I would say, was the last to re-discover this! Sages and Rishis during the ancient times used to time travel using their mind and this phenomenon was called 'Astral projection'. Did they use this capability to predict, the past and present of human beings which is termed "Nadi Jothidam"? It is said that the Seven Maharishis (sages) Agasthya, Kausika, Vyasa, Bohar, Brigu, Vasishtha and Valmiki had predicted the previous, presnt and future and then written life of each individual on leaves of a palm tree by their spiritual powers. Some believe it and others have a different view about this. These Nadi leaves were initially stored in the premises of Tanjore Saraswati Mahal of Tamilnadu State in India. The British rulers later showed interest in the Nadi leaves concerned with herbs and medicine, future prediction etc; but ironically left most of the Nadi prediction leaves to their loyal people. Some leaves get destroyed and some were auctioned during the British rule. Some Nadi leaves were anyhow retrieved and saved by the families of astrologers in Vaitheeswarankovil from The Tanjore Saraswati Mahal Library.

I guess that most of you would know about this. When a material body travels closer to the speed of light of 30,000 Km/s (1/10 the speed of light) then time dilation becomes important. A moving clock runs more slowly than one that is stationary with respect to the person observing the clocks. At normal speeds, the effect is very small, but as speeds approach those of the speed of light, the effect becomes more pronounced.

Length contraction is the observation that a moving object appears shorter than a stationary object. Like time dilation, length contraction is a consequence of the postulates of relativity. Length contraction and time dilation are related, and introduce a relation between length and time (or space and time, if you prefer)

When the object travels closer to speed of light Time slows down, length decreases in the direction of velocity and mass increases. Astral projection (or astral travel) is an esoteric interpretation of any form of out of body experience that assumes the existence of an "astral body" separate from the physical body, and capable of traveling outside it.

There is an old legend in Hinduism about king Kakudmi and his beautiful daughter Reavathi to convince that time dilation was known before Einstein relativity theory was put forward. According to Vedic calculations one Kalpa is 8.64 trillion earth years which is a day and a night for the creator Brahma. When they arrived, Brahma was listening to a musical performance by the Gandharvas, so they waited patiently until the performance was finished. Gandharvas were one time citizens of Kandahar, the second largest city in Afghanistan and excelled in Knowledge, Music and Dance. Taxila and Kandahar formed important centers of commerce and education for the empire of Ashoka the Great. In fact, Taxila was one of the first universities to be founded in India.

Kakudmi bowed humbly, made his request and presented his shortlist of candidates. Brahma laughed loudly, and explained that time runs differently on different planes of existence, and that during the short time they had waited in Brahma-loka to see him, 27 *catur*-Yugas (a cycle of four yugas, totaling 108 yugas, or) had passed on earth. Brahma said to Kakudmi, "O King, all those whom you may have decided within the core of your heart to accept as your son-in-law have died in the course of time. Twenty-seven catur-yugas have already passed. Those upon whom you may have already decided are now gone, and so are their sons, grandsons and other descendants. You cannot even hear about their names. You must therefore bestow this virgin gem (i.e. Revati) upon some other husband, for you are now alone, and your friends, your ministers, servants, wives, kinsmen, armies, and treasures, have long since been swept away by the hand of time" Brahamma recommended Balarama as a worthy husband for Revati. Only through such a legendary story the importance of time and Time dilation could be explained. Kakudmi and Reavati then returned to earth, which they regarded as having left only just a short while ago. They were shocked by the changes that had taken place. Not only had the landscape and environment changed, but over the intervening 27 *catur*-yugas. Similar stories also exist in the Middle East, appearing in the Arabian Nights.

In Modern Physics, space travel proves the Time dilation theory. If an astronaut starts his journey in space on 1st January in the year 2000 and travels in space for two years at a speed closer to light and returns to earth as per his clock on 2002, the date in the earth surface will not be the same as what his clock indicates. This is an example of Time Dilation, a concept of modern physics. As per Vedas Rishis initiated their capacity to travel in different time frames and experienced the happenings. This is like the Time machine story.

Photons behave like both a particle and a wave and many wonder what that means? It's true. Sometimes light acts like a wave, and other times it behaves like a little particle. This concept is derived from the Quantum theory. As the frequency of the particle, while the vibration increases, its Energy increases. In an atom when an orbiting electron around the nucleus moves from one energy level to another, it generates a photon (light) with energy equal to the difference in energy levels. In a similar way when a person meditates and moves to a higher energy level he behaves like the dual nature of particle when he moves to the seventh chakra level. This is the basic concept of Nirvana through meditation. When Ramana Maharishi attained Nirvana through intense meditation, a bright light emerged from his physical body.

Playing with energy levels is an art developed in Hinduism. Those who have developed that capacity, at times use it for good things like curing diseases but many abuse it and amass wealth. Prediction of what is going to happen is a common feature among such sadhus.

*   *   *

9

Idols in Hinduism

In business, the logo plays an important part in promoting a product. It is an easy way to identify the product and build allegience. The name of the logo becomes the symbol of the product and people identify it by the symbol. Symbols are often a quick way to communicate complex ideas. Religions, particularly esoteric ones, commonly employ a great amount of symbolism to represent their beliefs. There is a close similarity between the logo and symbols used in Hinduism and other religions. In Hinduism, the religious cult use it for worshiping without understanding the concept of the symbols used among Vaishnavites and Shaivites.

Some Temples in Sri Lanka

In many Hindu temples in Tamil Nadu and Sri Lanka the walls are painted in red and white stripes. Female energy (Sakthi) is represented by red and male energy (Sivam) by white colour. This the reason why Walls of Hindu temples are painted in red and white stripes alternatively whether it is a Shiva, Sakthi or Vishnu temple. It is a way of identifying the building as a Hindu temple. This is another form of symbolism. In the same way as the shape of the architecture of the Mosque, Buddhist Dagoba, and Christian church, help to identify the religion. The Mosque has crescent as a symbol and in the same way in Hinduism the Crescent is reflected as a symbol on Lord Siva's head. The waxing and waning phenomenon of the moon symbolizes the time cycle through which creation evolves from the beginning to the end. Since the Lord is the Eternal Reality, He is beyond time. Thus, the crescent moon is not his integral part but is only one of his ornaments.

When meditating or praying, people need a symbol or an idol to concentrate on. This symbol, whether a Cross, or Linga, chanting Aum is concentrated in the forehead. Idol identifies the different sects such as Vaishnavism, Saivism, Saktism, etc. In addition, there are the Sauras, who worship the Sun-God; Ganapatyas who worship Ganesh as supreme; and Kumaras who worship Skanda as the Godhead. These sects developed over a period of time in different regions in India under different rulers. Idols are not God and are only objects of reference. Over a period of time the legendary stories built about the idol by devotees, made people to believe them as God who fulfills their requests.

Many idols have family bondings and legends are created around the families, Nadarajar, Parvathy, Ganapathy, and Karthigeya (Murugan), people think are from one family for which Nadarajar is the father, Parvathy (Sakthi) the mother and the other two are the children. In reality it is not true but this is the only way the different concepts of these idols can be conveyed to a common man who is used to family life. Legendary stories were built by the devotees around the family of idols. That made it easier for people to understand the complex concepts. To explain the concept through objects held by the idol many hands were required, to make them believe that idols were supernatural and different from humans. People believed Karthigeya had six faces but it was not so. So is Elephant faced Ganapthy. The faces and the body structure of idols are not the same everywhere. If built on a stone or in a metal it looks different. Even in pictures, the picture of Nadarajar, Partvathy, Vishnu, Lakshimi, Saraswathy are different.

Hindus do not consider it a 'sin' in any manner to use icons, images, or linguistic symbols such as the sacred "Aum", Spear (Vale), Trident, etc to represent divinity. Hindus do worship idols, but so do Christians, Jews and even Muslims. Muslims believe (without proof) that the revered "black stone" (Alhajar Al-Aswad) is a special divine meteorite that pre-dates creation that fell at the foot of Adam and Eve. It is presently embedded in the southeastern corner of the Kaba. Muslims touch and kiss the black stone during Hajj but non-Muslims are strictly forbidden to even touch it. The pagan Arabs practiced polytheism. They worshipped nature, stones, angels and demons. Particular reverence was accorded the three 'daughters of God', and various national, local and family idols. Each tribe gave allegiance to a special protector: one God to whom it turned in times of distress. Our modern altars may have had their beginnings in the stone worship of the ancients. One stone still holds a revered spot in the Arab heart. This is the stone that fell from paradise at the fall of Adam. Pure white it was and housed in a temple built by Seth, Adam's son, until a great flood ravaged the land, destroyed the temple, and buried it under the mud and debris. Before Muhammad appeared, the Kaaba was surrounded by 360 idols, and every Arab house had its God.

The important symbol among Shaivites is the **Linga** or **Lingam** (Sanskrit word for "symbol") is the symbol of the God Shiva and the form in which he is most commonly worshipped. The phallic symbol is the main object of worship in Shaivite temples and homes throughout India and the world. The Linga is a simple stylized phallus that nearly always rests on pedestal of a stylized **Yoni,** or female sex organ. Together, the Scholars believe that the Linga was revered by some non-Aryan people of India since antiquity, and short, cylindrical pillars with rounded tops have been found in Harappan remains. The Vedic Aryans appear to have disapproved of linga worship, but literary and artistic evidence shows that it was firmly established by the 1st-2nd century AD. The Linga's form became important during the Gupta period, so that in later periods its original phallic realism was to a considerable degree lost. Iconography of Shaivism with the phallic linga treated as Shiva's symbol. The Linga is depicted in sculpture and paintings as resting in the yoni as a cylinder in a spouted dish. The two symbols together represent the eternal process of creation and regeneration. The scientific explanation of Linga is the source of creating life in when it combines with yoni. Both energies are vital for creation and considered vital for the existence of the human race.

The three bands one could see on the foreheads of the gods and goddesses worshiped by Shaivites. These three bands are worn by the Shaivites and the other religions in that family. This symbol is called three bands. In the Shaivite religion, naturally ash becomes the symbol and could be seen as a sign in the forehead. The meaning behind the ash band is to make the humans realize that ultimate state of the body is that when one dies the body turns into ash, when the body is cremated or buried.

The symbol of "Trisula" is usually a Hindu-Buddhist religious symbol. Based on the Sanskrit terms Shula (spear, lance) and tri (three), the trishula or trident has three sharp points rather than one. In extension, or perhaps even being the origin of this symbol, also a naturally occuring three-pronged branch from a tree is called trishula. The trishula is one of the most popular symbols of God Shiva. In the Tibetan tradition, it is also a (magical) weapon carried by some of the protective deities.

Although more common in the Hinduism than in the Buddhist tradition, the trident occurs in depictions of deities from both schools, always symbolizing any of the concepts connected with the number three. In Buddhism, these are Buddha, Dharma and Sangha—in Hinduism the three gunas, the three nadis, or the three gods of the Trimurti namely Bramma, Vishnu and Siva.

They are commonly said to represent various trinities namely creation, maintenance and destruction, past, present and future, the three gunas. It also represents the place where the three main nadis or energy channels meet at the brow. Shushmana, the central one, continues upward to the 7th chakra, or energy center, while the other two ends at the brow, there the 6th chakra is located.

In Nepal, the trishaw is the election symbol of the Communist party of Nepal. In Sri Lanka and South India, Trisula is identified as Vairavar, the guardian to protect from evil. The shape of the symbol identifies it as a weapon in the war to kill the enemy. In many villages and in the cemeteries in Sri Lanka and South India Trisula is displayed and people boil rice with milk to show as a gratitude for protecting the people from evil. This practice exists through tradition and a lemon is pierced on the sharp edges of the Trisula.

Hindus pay so much of importance to symbols Hinduism at its core maintains that there is one God and many see it in different ways. This God is formless and is beyond the limitations of comprehension. This is the basis on which many of the great sages meditate on this Supreme Being that is beyond any contours. So why are there so many forms? It is very difficult to comprehend

God in a natural form, leave alone loving that God and worshiping with devotion. The simple minds of humans needed a way by which they could worship Boundless God in a fairly simplified manner. But at the same time it should not contradict the basis that the God is beyond form in any way. Hinduism maintains that because of the abundant Grace, God revealed itself in the Holy symbols for the humans and other creatures to worship. These symbols are easy to comprehend by the minds of the normal human beings, but at the same time they are just symbols than objects themselves, which means that they symbolically indicate the one Power that is God, which is beyond the exploration of knowledge.

In meditation the a symbol of choice is brought to focus in the forehead, and concentrated on, while reciting "Aum Namasivaya" mantra or any other mantra in the mind. As the concentration becomes stronger and stronger without the interference of other thoughts the symbol disappears. The symbol used need not belong to a religion like Christianity. In a way these Hindu symbols are abstract representation of God. These are quite closer to the ideal as they form a bridge between the formless one and the mind that expects a form. The simpler minds benefit better if the God could be correlated with the day to day lives they interact with. God certainly grants grace for the up liftmen of creation, God appeared in various forms during various occasions to bless devotees either in valorous or joyful or yogic postures. There are numerous of these forms that Hindus worship in their temples, which are built in a gigantic manner with the patronage of various emperors that stand as the glorious homes of art and architecture. The three prongs of the trishula represent Shiva's three aspects of: creator, preserver destroyer as well as the three Shaktis (powers): will, action, wisdom.

The symbol used by worshippers of Vishnu is Namam. The Y shaped namam with a red line in the center carries a meaning. The white line symbolizes the male (Vishnu) and the red line symbolizes Luximi, wife of Vishnu and the female energy both combined without separation forms, in the namum. This is another reason why the walls of the temples of any God are painted in Red and white bands depicting the two forms of the male and female energies responsible for the creation of human life.

The red and white lines in a temple walls is a sign to identify Hindu temples. In the Iyengar caste, worshippers of Vishnu have the namam in different form. Sri Vaishnava iyengars wear an elaborate Y shaped or U shaped white mark covering their foreheads, with a red line vertically down the centre — y or u depends on whether he belongs to the Thengalai or the Vadagalai sect. The phrase Namam also represents the coarse white soil found at the deeper layer of earth, which is used as the powder to wear a flame shaped mark. The (*Path of the father*) Ayyavazhi people wore this Namam, starting from the central point between the eyebrows, going straight up near the top edge of the forehead. The flame shape represents Aathman. The symbol of Ayyavazhi is a lotus carrying a flame-shaped white Namam

Murugan is considered as the guardian god of Kucinich (Mountain) land; hence Murugan temples are located mostly in hills. Kucinich land is the area where hunters live and they use the spear as their weapon to kill animals. The spear is the symbol of worship for hunters in Thailand and Vodkas in Sri Lanka. Instead of a deity, the Spear (Vel) is used in popular temples in Sri Lanka. The legendary story tells how He fell in love with a Veddha girl called Valli in the Southern Sri Lankan area and married her as His second wife. The marriage of Theyvayanai to Murugan signifies that the Atman (Soul represented by Theyvayanai) seeks to unite with the Brahmatman (represented by Murugan) and the marriage of Valli signifies that at times Brahmatman seeks the union of Aathman. Later commentators and the Saiva Siddhanda Philosophers have interpreted the two consorts of Murugan as being His inherent energy. Theyvayanai is Energy of Action (Kriya-Sakthi) and Valli is Energy of Desire (Iccha-Sakthi). But in actual worship however, the Supreme place of honour is reserved for Murugan although He accompanies Theyvayanai and

Valli The first wife was Theyvayani. The Vel is also refers to the elephant in archaic and poetic usage. This seems to be because the frontal profile of an elephant (with the long trunk) is similar to a spear. The philosophical explanation of the shape of the spear is Sharp intelligence with a broader outlook and deeper thinking power.

It is also said that Theyvayanai and Valli are daughters of Vishnu, the maternal uncle of Murugan and by His marriage, Murugan acts as a link between the Vaishnavaites (worshippers of Vishnu) and the Saivaites (worshippers of Siva).

*   *   *

10

Rituals & Science

Rituals are actions that produce results. The methods are defined in rituals and they are linked with methods, mantras, bajans and beliefs. The process varies from ritual to ritual and the purpose for which it is performed. Some rituals are followed after fasting. Hindus believe that through various rituals they could get the blessings from God. Hindu religious practices center on the importance of fulfilling the duties associated both with one's social position and one's stage of life. With regard to the latter, traditional Hindus are expected to pass through four stages during the course of their life, which are childhood, youth, middle age, and old age.

1. *Brahmacharga,* which takes place during the school years, is focused on acquiring knowledge and developing character. It is the unmarried part of life.

2. *Grahasstha*, the middle years, is focused on worldly pursuits and pleasures such as marriage, family and career; This is more sex oriented

3. *Vanaprastha*, when one's children reach adulthood, is a time of increased focus on spiritual advancement; Experience increases the desire for spirituality and the rejection of materialistic life develops.

4. *Sanngasu*, in the last years of life, one may abandon the world entirely for a life of contemplation.

In each of these stages of life rituals are traditionally performed and some of the major Hindu practices and items used in the rituals are described below.

"**Puja**" is a religious ritual in many religions based on a set procedure, the time it is carried out, and the mantras used in the Pujas. Some Hindus perform Puja every morning after bathing and dressing, before taking any food or drink. Puja is seen as a way of relating humans to the domain and actions of the divine, and can be performed for anything considered divine, from Linga, Vishnu, Sakthi, or a holy tree. Pujas vary for each deity and the occasion during which it is performed.

Rituals are most common during special event like Ear piercing, Teaching the alphabet the first time to the child, Shaving the head to get rid of the hair with which the child was born, age attaining ceremony, wedding and death. These are usually performed by individuals rather than Brahmins and are conducted within the family. The procedure varies in every religious cult and among caste and area.

Samskars are tendencies inherited from previous births and begin even before a child is born. **Garbhadana** (conception) is the fervent prayer for a child. This is done in order to fulfill the parental duties to continue the race. **Punsavana** (fetus protection) is performed during the third or fourth month of pregnancy before the fetus is conscious. The prayers help to invoke divine qualities in the child. Valaikappu (satisfying the craving of the pregnant mother) is similar to a baby shower. It is performed during the seventh month, and prayers are offered for healthy physical and mental growth of the child. **Jatakarma** is performed at the birth of the child. It is done to welcome the child into the family. **Mantras,** or verse prayers, are recited for a healthy, long life. The naming ceremony, or **namakarna,** is done according to scriptural procedures. Also at this time, the child is taken outdoors for the first time. This is performed at the age of four months. The final samskar for childhood is the **annaprasana**, or giving the child solid food for the first time.

For boys in the upper three castes, a second birth ceremony is performed. This is known as the thread ceremony. During this ritual, boys eat a final meal with their mothers, and then are introduced to manhood. After this ceremony, boys are expected to eat with the men and take on more responsibilities. They "die" of their young self, and are "born" into their new, older self.

Marriage **(vivaha)** is the middle age passage. The Hindu marriage is much more than an exchange of vows and rings. Before and during the nuptials, many rites are performed in the presence of family deities. These rites show the importance of a strong bond between a husband and wife. The marriage is considered incomplete without the blessings of a spiritual or divine element. The final rite of passage is death. In the Hindu tradition, individuals are cremated and special rites are done to ensure a good after life. In the olden days the wife joins the husband in the funeral pyre (Suttee) but now this is prohibited by law.

Other special rituals include the **"Griha"** which means in Sanskrit-Abode'. These are domestic rites that are taught by priests for use in the home. They celebrate new and full moons, changing of the seasons, first fruits of the harvest, the building of a new house, birth of a son, and the above-mentioned, and rites of passage.

In all rituals, the five "pancha boothas"(The five sources of energies) are involved. Showing the flame to the deity is an important part of the ritual. Light symbolizes knowledge, and darkness—ignorance. The

Lord is the "Knowledge Principal" who is the source, the enlivener and the illuminator of all knowledge. Hence light is worshiped as the Lord himself. Knowledge removes ignorance just as light removes darkness. Also knowledge is a lasting inner wealth by which all outer achievement can be accomplished. Hence we make light through burning camphor or oil. On every Saturday of the Tamil month of September rituals are performed by burning gingili seeds and oil to the God of Saturn to overcome evil. Each planet is allocated a colour, gem, grain and metal to signify the importance of nature. For the planet Saturn blue sapphire, Sesame (Gingili), Iron and steel are allocated. Saturn is a very slow moving planet and takes two and half years to cross one sign of 30 degrees. Unless it is a new moon or full moon day, generally during all Saturdays, the atmospheric pressure is minimal and causes lethargic attitude in most of us who suffer during the seven and a half year period of Saturn. In South Indian temples burning gingili seeds in oil on Saturdays is a method that is supposed to relieve the ill effects of Saturn, viz. by inhaling the gingili Carbon, the ventricles take it directly to the brain and the chemical reaction caused in the brain releases the excessive radiation of Saturn from the brain, through the seven visible holes in the face itself — i.e. nostrils, ear, eyes and mouth. In addition, the skull punch or the focal point, (from where brain waves are emitted) also ventilates

Saturn's radiations. Saturn's rays are, presumably, thick containing more iron substance/iodine.

Rituals are developed traditionally. Camphor is burned in Temples and the scientific explanation for this is that the smoke coming out of the burning of camphor, acts as disinfectant to prevent spreading of viruses among the crowd. The shape of the flame is almost triangular with a thin apex and thicker at the center. The philosophical explanation of this is that man should have a broader outlook and sharper mind. The fire in the form of lamp, is one of the five pancha boothas to bow down to knowledge as the greatest of all forms of wealth. Fire brings in brightness and eradicates darkness. Water, one of the pancha boothas is commonly used for purification in all rituals. To signify the Earth, a square like platform is set up to burn the fire. Air surrounding the ritual area is purified through mantras and the smoke from "**Sambrani**" a kind of incense when burnt generates fragrant smell and acts as disinfectant and overpowers the bad smell generated through the sweat from the crowd.

Like the Muslims during Ramadhan season, Hindus observe fasting during festival season such as Kandha Sashti and Sivarathiri. The rest and change of diet during fasting is very good for the digestive system and the entire body. The more you indulge the senses, the more they make their demands. Observing fasts like "Kandashasti" help us to cultivate control over our senses, sublimate our desires and guide our minds to be poised and be at peace. Fasting should not make us weak, irritable or create an urge to indulge later. The Bhagavad-Gita urges us to eat appropriately — neither too less nor too much.

In India one of the most common offerings in a temple is a coconut and flowers. It is also offered on occasions like weddings, festivals, the use of a new vehicle, bridge, house etc. It is offered in the sacrificial fire whilst performing homa. The coconut is broken and placed before the Lord. It is later distributed as prasaada. The fiber covering of the dried coconut is removed except for a tuft on the top. The marks on the coconut make it look like the head of a human being. The coconut is broken, symbolizing the breaking of the ego. The juice within, representing the inner tendencies (vaasanas) is offered along with the white kernel — the mind, to the Lord. A mind thus purified by the touch of the Lord is used as prasaada (a holy gift).

In the traditional abhishekha ritual done in all temples and many homes, several materials are poured over the deity like milk, curd, honey, tender coconut water, sandal paste, holy ash etc. Each material has a specific significance of bestowing certain benefits on the worshippers. Tender coconut water is used in abhisheka rituals since it is believed to bestow spiritual growth to the seeker.

The coconut also symbolizes selfless service. Every part of the tree — the trunk, leaves, fruit, coir etc are used in innumerable ways like thatches, mats, tasty dishes, oil, soap etc. It takes in even salty water from the earth and converts it into sweet nutritive water that is especially beneficial like saline, to sick people. It is used in the preparation of many ayurvedic medicines and in other alternative medicinal therapies.

The marks on the coconut are even thought to represent the three-eyed Lord Shiva and therefore considered to be a means to fulfill our desires. "Shaanti," meaning "peace", is a natural state of being. Disturbances are created either by ourselves or others. For example, peace already exists in a place until someone makes a noise. This word is frequently used by those who are involved in do meditation. Silence is a must for concentration in meditation.

However, peace within or without seems very hard to attain because it is covered by our own agitations. A rare few manage to remain peaceful within even in the midst of external agitation and troubles. To invoke peace, we chant prayers. By chanting prayers, troubles end and peace is experienced internally, irrespective of the external disturbances. All such prayers end by chanting shaanti thrice. We chant shaanti thrice to emphasize our intense desire for peace. All obstacles, problems and sorrows originate from three sources. May peace alone prevail. Hence shaanti is chanted thrice. It is chanted aloud the first time, addressing the unseen forces. It is chanted softer the second time, directed to our immediate surroundings and those around, and softest the last time as it is addressed to oneself.

Towards the every ritualistic worship, aarati is performed. This is always accompanied by the ringing of the bell and sometimes by singing, playing of musical instruments and clapping. This is one of the sixteen steps of the puja ritual. It is referred to as the lighted lamp in the right hand, which we wave in a clockwise circling movement to light the entire form of the Lord.

Each part is revealed individually and also the entire form of the Lord. As the light is waved we either do mental or loud chanting of prayers or simply behold the beautiful form of the Lord, illumined by the lamp. At the end of the aarati we place our hands over the flame and then gently touch our eyes and the top of the head.

We have seen and participated in this ritual from our childhood. Let us find out why we do this aarati? Aarati is often performed with camphor which has a special spiritual significance. Camphor when lit, burns itself out completely without leaving any trace of it. It represents our inherent tendencies (vaasanas), another important aspect of rituals itself.

The "Kumbam", a silver vessel decorated with coloured threads, silk cloth, mango leaves and a coconut placed on banana leaf with rice is called a "kumbam". A lamp is lit next to it and the Panchaboothas are represented in this set up. It is used in Hindu pujas especially in homams and all rituals. The Kumbam resembles a human head where the coconut plays an important part.

Worshiping in Hinduism has significance. In Tamil culture, holding both hands together with fingers pointing up, is a way of welcoming and they call "Vannakam" in Tamil. The same style is adopted in praying in front of an idol.

*   *   *

11

Ganapathy worship &
the Temples for Ganapathy

Ganapathy

There are many major deities in Hinduism. Each brings forward a philosophical concept for human being with a hidden scientific explanation. Ganapathy worship is for promoting wisdom. When any new venture is undertaken, Ganapathy is worshipped first. He is worshipped to prevent and remove obstacles. It is also believed that failure to worship Ganapathy will lead to problems. The elephant has the strength to remove any heavy objects that block progress.

Many legendary stories explain the creation of Ganapathy. The stories are questionable. Ganapathy was created from the body of Ambal by herself. She made him her body-guard. In a battle, his head was cut off. Siva fixed an elephant's head onto the body. So he became named as Gajaanana. Ganesha emerged a distinct deity in clearly recognizable form in the 4th and 5th centuries AD, during the Gupta period, although he inherited traits from Vedic and pre-Vedic precursors. It is generally assumed that Ganesha was brought to Tamilnadu by Siruththondar from Vaathapi in the North. Siruthondar was the army commander of Pallava king Narasimha Varman. He was called Paramsothy. He went North and fought the battle against Challukiya king at Vaathapi and won the battle. When he returned to Tamil Nadu he brought a statue of Ganesh from Vaathapi. His popularity rose quickly, and he was formally included among the five primary deities in the 9th century. Thiruchengattankudi is mentioned in Sivakamiyin Sabatham because Pallava Commander Paranjothi, after conquering Vathabi got permission from Pallava king Narasimha Varman to go back to his native Chozha land to become Sivanadiyar and afterwards he was known as Siruthondar Nayanar. Though name "Ganapathy" appears in Rigveda, he is not the same God who is worshipped as elephant-headed God today. "Gana" represents a clan and "Pati" is considered chieftain. In Vedic times, image worship did not exist and "Ganapathy" stood for Brihaspati or Brahmin. This God of wisdom has two wives, "Siddhi" and "Buddhi." Sidlhi is achievement and Buddhi is intellect. This is misinterpreted by some Hindus. The Elephant has these two characteristics.

Before commencing the ritualistic worship, rice (grain) is spread over the seat on which the idol of Ganesh is to be installed. Either a fistful or a mound of rice is used, depending on the local custom. On invocation of Ganapathy and his ritualistic worship, energy is generated in the idol. This energy saturates the rice on which the idol is placed. If there are two strings of a musical instrument (a stringed musical instrument) of the same frequency, when sound is generated by one the same is generated by the other. This we call resonance. Similarly, when frequencies of energy are generated in the rice below the idol, this energy is transmitted to the rice stored in the house. Thus one can eat rice saturated with energy as a sacrament of food (prasadam) throughout the year.

When performing each of the following rituals a particular mantra is recited. Each animal in nature, exhibits a special philosophical concept. Especially elephant has a good memory power. The big head of Ganesha's symbolism signifies think big. The two large ears explain that listening is vital in life. It develops knowledge. Hence first listen to what others say and think analytically. The two small eyes for a big head is something which is peculiar and disproportionate. Although the eyes are small it implies that concentration through observation is vital. The symbol carries an axe to break away the bond of attachment in life. Attachment slows progress. The rope he carries is to pull you nearer to the highest goal and prevent you from moving away from your objectives. The small mouth implies that one should talk less and show capability in action. The trunk explains high efficiency and adaptability. Big belly is to swallow the sins committed by human beings and peacefully digest the good and bad in life. The sweet Modhakam is a reward for achievement. One broken tusk explains the sacrifice made to write fast when Viayasar was dictating the Mahabaratha fast. For a big animal, the small mouse is disproportionate, but it has a meaning. The mouse can travel fast to overcome obstacles. Different explanations are given about the symbolism of Ganesh. The bottom line is, that it contains tremendous amount of energy that leads to a successful happy life.

Ganesh is the Lord of success and destroyer of evils and obstacles. He is also worshipped as the God of education, knowledge, wisdom and wealth. Before starting to write in examinations, interviews or writing reports the symbol of Ganesh is written on the top of the paper. Hindu students believe in this procedure. People believe that he guides you and makes your project a success. In temples, the puja is done first for Ganapthy and then only to the other deities. In fact, Ganesha is one of the five prime Hindu deities (Brahma, Vishnu, Shiva and Durga being the other four)

There is significance in the Ganesha form. Ganesha's head symbolizes the *Aatman* or the soul, which is the ultimate supreme reality of human existence, and his human body signifies *Maya* or the earthly existence of human beings. The elephant head denotes wisdom and its trunk represents AUM, the sound symbol of cosmic reality. In his upper right hand Ganesha holds a goad, which helps him to propel mankind forward on the eternal path and remove obstacles from the way. The noose in Ganesha's left hand is a gentle implement to capture all difficulties. The broken tusk that Ganesha holds like a pen in his lower right hand is a symbol of sacrifice, which he broke for writing the Mahabharata. The rosary in his other hand suggests that the pursuit of knowledge should be continuous. The Modakam (sweet) he holds in his trunk indicates that one must discover the sweetness of the *Atman*. His fan-like ears convey that he is all ears to our petitions. The snake that runs round his waist represents energy in all forms. And he is humble enough to ride the lowest of creatures, a mouse.

Gaja is found on the seals discovered at sites (like Harappa and Mohenjo-Daro of the Indus Valley Civilization (3000 BC-1700 BC). Some scholars believe that by that time elephants had been tamed and domesticated, and used for peaceful and possibly for other purposes. When Alexander the Great tried to invade India through Indus valley he was amazed at the elephants used in the battle field. That was the first time he saw elephants. In the Vedas, there is no direct reference to elephants. But during Vedic period when Alexander came to India from Greece to the Indus valley he was surprised to see the power of the elephants used in war.

Ganesha is also the destroyer of vanity, selfishness and pride. He is the personification of the material universe in all its various magnificent manifestations. The very purpose of Ganesha's big belly is to swallow everything, which comes in front of us. It doesn't mean that we eat a lot. It does not matter, if the event, the situation, the problem, the dialogue or the conversation is pleasant or unpleasant, just accept and swallow it, hear everything with wide open ears. Do not react to it. Let us keep quiet and just swallow the words! Learn to look into any matter very minutely with the small eyes. Smell it again and again with the big trunk like an elephant. Then whatever may be of any use, of any help, of any assistance, just keep only that and throw away the rest of it. It is said that the elephant will swallow the innermost part of a coconut and throw away the outside shell, However, when mangoes are given; it throws away the inner seed and eats only the pulp and the external skin! What a wonderful understanding!

To worship Lord Ganesh is to confine in concentration, contemplation, and finally abide in the supreme or the blessedness or the absolute, by focusing the mind initially upon individual level and then from individual to cosmic level. When we keep on persuading and observing this science of management of the self, every day, systematically, scientifically, regularly, without fail and with interest, we will definitely win the grace of Lord Ganesh. We receive and achieve Riddhi and Siddhi & nothing will be impossible because in the word impossible there lies the, nothing will be impossible because in the word impossible there lays the word possible, too!

Another popular aspect of Ganesh worship in some parts of Sri Lanka can be observed along the main roads, especially in the North-Central Province, where his statue is placed near trees and worshiped by travelers so that they may have a safe journey. A typical example is Murugandi Ganesh temple in A9 highway in Vanni. The ritual usually consists of breaking a coconut in his name, and offering a coin etc.

In predominantly Tamil areas as well as in upcountry estates, a black stone or a black stone-statue of God Pillaiyar (Ganesh) is placed at the foot of trees at certain places, venerated in a similar manner and this God is also known as Gana Deviyo among Singhalese. According to Hindu believers, Gana Deviyo had been commanded by God Shiva to stand by a roadside and it is this command that the Gana Deviyo is faithfully adhering to. Vows made to Gana Deviyo seeking his protection are followed by boiling of milk and offering it to the God seeking protection and grace from Him. In the Jaffna, Pillaiyar was regarded as the "guardian of the crops" and many shrines were erected by the agriculturists in the neighborhoods of their fields and are a common deity in Vanni area in the north, which is predominantly an agricultural area. According to local tradition, a temple dedicated to Ganesha was erected at Inuvil, in Jaffna, by Karunakara Thondaiman, the commander of Kulottunga Chola I (1070-1118 AD), and it is now known as Karunakara Pillaiyar Temple in Inuvil.

In the mountainous area of Nuwera Eliya, one finds such Ganesh small shrines, located at road crossings, often under trees. The statues display the typical South Indian style (black colored by cult smoke, dressed in a piece of tissue). Some colorful folk statues of Ganesh are also located scattered near road crossings in jungle regions between Anuradhapura and Polonnaruwa. The main reason is that paddy and sugarcane cultivators believe that Ganesh will protect the farm from destruction by elephants.

Other Ganesh representations in south of Lanka are much older ones. They can be seen in some Buddhist temples, where they are warily displayed. Some are mural paintings, with other Hindu deities (Vishnu, Indra, Kartthikeya), paying homage to the Buddha. One is in a Dambulla temple Cave, and another one in a cave of the Alu Vihara temple. Other statues: one small white standing Ganesh can be found in a Buddhist shrine at Embekke Devala located in Kandy and dedicated to the god Kataragama, built around 1370 AD. The best and biggest is hidden in an ancient part of the Lankatilaka temple, both near Kandy. There are other such ancient Ganesh representations existing in other places too.

The only temple which openly displays Ganesh is the well-known Kelaniya temple in a near suburb of Colombo. There, on the southern wall, a large sculpture of the benevolent God is displayed. He is seated on His huge rat.

Near Mihintale, the stupa Kantaka Cetinga is surrounded by a decorative frieze which inscriptions say to date from the 1st or 2nd century A.D. On this frieze, the elephant-headed god is undoubtedly carved. Indeed, one can see a twofold Gana procession moving towards an elephant-headed personage with a left-turned trunk. We can be sure that this is a Ganapathi representation, despite the antiquity of the frieze.

We could remember some good old stone Ganesh statues in the National Museum (Colombo); however, we regret that no information is given about their age and the place where they were found. On the other hand, two best pieces, one stone-made, one bronze-made (both from the 12th century), are presented in the excellent Polonnaruwa Museum. In the catalogue of the exposition in Paris describes a large splendid sitting bronze Ganesh from the 11th century (Polonnaruwa period, which has been found in the Shiva temple in 1960. The author writes that this unique specimen would be on display in the Anuradhapura museum. According to the picture, no doubt that this piece is the Ganesh now displayed in Polonnaruwa. The Ganesh statue in the Raja Maha Vihara in Kelaniya is very noticeable.

There are several ancient Sinhala texts written for beginners during the time of Pirivena education prior to the establishment of schools by the British. One such early book is 'Ganadevi Hella'. As the name indicates, 'Ganadevi Hella' was a collection of verses referring to the Hindu God Ganesh, popularly known as Ganadevio in Sinhala. There are 49 verses in this book. A typical verse in the book popular even today reads: There are several Pillaiyar (Ganesh) Temples in Northern area, Jaffna. To name some of them:

Chulipuram: Kannaikothikakkai Pillaiyar temple

Inuvil: Karunakara Pillaiyar temple — A popular old temple

Manipay: Maruthady   Vinayagar   temple — A popular old temple

Murukandi: Murukandi Pillaiyar temple in Vanni, patronized by travelers on highway A9. Many years ago, in the trunk of a Tree, on the road side, the symbol of Ganapathy appeared.

Nallur Kailasa Pillaiyar and the Ganesh temple **Veiyilugandha** Pillayar are another Pillayar temples with an old heritage located near the Nallur temple in Jaffna. The rays of the sun enter the main shrine called Moolasthana of Veiyilugandha Pillayar, hence it got this name. These two act as Guardians of Nallur Temple.

Neervely: Arasakesari Pillaiyar temple

Neeraviyadi Pillayar temple

Alaveddy: Kumbalavalai Pillaiyar temple

Batticaloa: Mamamanga Pillaiyar temple

Colombo: Shri Muthu Vinayaga temple, Chetty Street

Bambalapitiya: New Kathiresan temple

Kandy: Selva Vinayaka temple

Kataragama: Manikka Vinayaka temple and many more

GANESH TEMPLES IN SRI LANKA

India, has the highest Hindu population of 828 Million, 80.5 % of the total Indian population. Himachal Pradesh has the highest Hindu population and Tamil Nadu has 55 Million Hindus with many Saiva temples. It is estimated that in Sri Lanka there are about 4800 temples in the island. There are about 2495 temples in the Eastern province and about 775 temples in up country. The Northern province has the largest number of temples of about 2495.

Nallur is one time the capital of a Hindu kingdom in the Jaffna Peninsula and the Murugan temple as the most popular one located few miles from Jaffna town. Surrounding this temple there are many important Ganapthy temples as protectors, the concept on which the previous kings who ruled the Jaffna Kingdom built temples for Lord Shiva's family. Nallur Sivan temple, followed by the Veerakali Amman temple representing Sakthi and Kailasa Pillayar Kovil in the South, Veiyilugandha Pillayar Temple in the East, surround the Nallur Murugan temple. All these temples were badly destroyed when the Portuguese invaded Jaffna.

Neeraviadi Pillayar—Each temple has a history behind it. In addition to these temples the most popular ones with a legend are:

In 948 A.D, Chief Minister to Chola Kulangai Aarya, called Bhuvanekabhahu, first built a temple for Lord Kumaran in Kurukkal Valavu in Nallur. In 1450, Senbahap Perumal, the General of Parakramabahu came from Anuradhapura to conquer Jaffna, and destroyed the temple. Regretting his action, in 1457, he tried to make amends by building the temple in Muthirai Chanthai, a few kilometers from the present temple. During the Portuguese invasion, in 1619, it was again destroyed. In 1734 it was constructed again in Muthirai Chanthai.

Kailasa pillayar Kovil is located walking distance south of Nallur temple. When Nallur temple was destroyed this Pillayar temple too was also destroyed. The Pillayar statue along with Ambal and Perumal statues were hidden from the main shrine of the temple. The aim if the invaders were to stop the Hindus from practicing the religion and to plunder the wealth of the temple. When the Nallur temple was renovated, Kailasapillayar temple too was renovated and the pujas for Pillayar recommenced. Ten days festivals now take place starting on the full moon day in April. The Pillayar temples surrounding the Murugan temples were destroyed.

Veiyilugandha Pillayar is another Pillayar temple with an old heritage located in the East, where the rays of the sun enter the main shrine called Moolasthanam. The meaning of the name of the temple signifies its exposure to the rays of the sun. There are several explanations given why the temple to got its name. Since the idol was brought from India, the name of the idol linking the name of the village from where it was brought was given to the temple. Even when it rained, the sunrays fell on the Pillayar statue, hence the name was given. 'Muthirai Santhai' (Market) is the focal point at the city layout of the ancient Nallur Rajasthani. The piece of land that falls close to the Veiyilugandha Pillayar is called Kottai Vaasal (Fort entrance). Another piece of land in the Southeast Regions is called kottai adi. The fact that a piece of land called by the name `Kottai adi' is near the Veiyilugandha Pillayar temple gives room to believe that the Eastern entrance of the Nallur Rajsthani must have been in that region only. Veiyilugandha Pillayar temple and Sattanadhar temple are equidistance from 'Muthirai Santhai'.

Considering the fact that 'Muthirai Santhai' was the centre of Nallur Rajathani, we can reasonably contend that the temples which were in all the four directions must have been somewhat at equidistance from the market place. The temple of Veiyilugandha Pillayar, who is the defending God of farmers is located in the area adjacent to Semmani which is full of agricultural fields.

NEERAVIYADI PILLAYAR TEMPLE.

This is an old temple not too far from Jaffna Hindu College. The tank next to the temple is completely neglected and filled with shrubs. A Sithar named Kadayil swami passed away in the area near the temple. No one knows the date or place of his birth, the details of his parentage or even the name given to him. However, it is known that Kadai Swami hailed from the state of Karnataka, that he was called Swami Mukti Ananda and that he had mastered English, Sanskrit, Kannada and Tamil.

MARUTAHDI PILLAYAR KOVIL:

This is one of the popular Ganapthy temples in Manipay, a town located not too far from Jaffna. However, the town is a Christian dominated one because of the influence of The American Mission in the past and also because of Jaffna College and Uduvil Girls College. Maruthadi Pillayar became popular among the Hindus living in Manipay and villages surrounding Manipay. The temple festival takes place for 18 days. The car festival takes place on the day of the Tamil New year.

The tree Marutham is the temple tree and the legend says that long time back Ganapthy appeared as a statue in the Marutham Tree, hence the temple got its name. It is located opposite the famous Green Hospital and the patients worship there.

Inuvil Pararasasekara Vinayakar temple is one of the sacred Hindu temples in Jaffna. Inuvil village is located a few miles from Jaffna Town on the Jaffna Palaly road. The history of the temple goes back to the period of Ariya Chakkarawarthees in Jaffna. It was during the rule of Ariya Chakkaravarthees that the worship of Ganesha became popular in Jaffna. There is evidence that several Vinayaka temples such as Karunakara Pillayar temple, Paralai Vinayakar temple, Veyil Uhantha Pillaiyar temple and Kailasa Pillayar temple were established during this period. Similarly, it can be concluded that Pararasasekara Vinayakar temple, too, was erected during the rule King Pararasasekaran.

According to a verse of ancient times, King Pararasasekaran, who belonged to the eleventh generation of the Ariya Chakaravarthies, had worshipped at this temple. A picture in the main Mandapam of the temple, depicts King Pararasasekaran worshipping at the temple in the company of his ministers.

The main deity installed in the sanctum sanctorum (Karbagraham) is the Vinayakar. This statue was made by reputed Indian sculptors and installed there. The

Poojas are performed according to agama principles and traditions.

There are separate shrines for Gaja Luxmi, Santhana Gopalar, Valli Theivanai Sametha Subramaniyar, Bala Ganapathy, Bala Murugan, Four Samaya Kuravars, Nava Graham, Vairavar, Maha Luxmi and Sandeswarar.

The annual temple festival commences in the month of Vaikasi in the auspicious hour of Sathaya Natchthiram with the hoisting of the flag. It is a 9 day festival. The chariot festival is on the tenth day, while the water cutting ceremony is on the eleventh day—in the punarpoosa natchathiram. Prior to the hoisting of the flag, the Kodi Kavi composed by Umapathy Sivacharyar is recited.

The first Kumbabishekam is said to have been in 1939. The second was in January 1961. Raja Gopura Kumbhabishekam was on 1972. There was another in 1984, followed by another in 1997.

The story of Pillayar recitation is performed according to Hindu traditions on the days that Vinayakar Shasty fast is observed. This tradition has been continued in the temple for years, because this will help devotees to imbibe faith in Lord Ganesha. Devotees are not enlightened about the scientific concept of Pillayar deity.

* * *

12

Shivalinga Worship

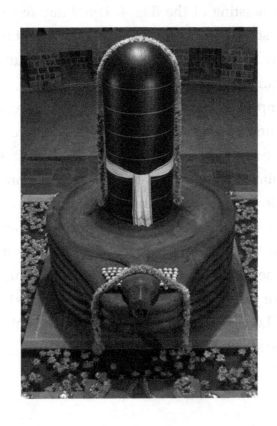

SHIVALINGA SYMBOLIZES MALE ENERGY.

Shiva, the lord of the erect Phallus, is traced to the ithyphallic figure of Indus Valley civilization or to the phallic images found more generally in prehistoric India. Lord Shiva's other form is 'Ardhanariswara, half man and half woman. Lord Shiva, with his consort Parvati, is always in a celestial dance of procreation and destruction of the worlds.

PHYSICAL ATTRIBUTES IF LINGA

a. **Ganga** : Just as the sun is the focal point of the solar system and the soul that of the body, the focal point of divine consciousness in every object and pure particles is purity. The flow from Ganga is assumed to be pure. Ganga flows from Shiva's head. This is called the descent of the Ganga from Shiva's head. Since the river Ganga has a fraction of the principle of the spiritual Ganga, no matter how polluted it becomes, its purity is perpetually retained. Hence, when compared to any other water in the world, the water from the Ganga is the purest. This is realized not only by those who can perceive the subtle dimension but also by scientific researchers.

b. **Moon** : Shiva wears the Chandra (moon) on his forehead. The point where the three frequencies — affection, mercifulness and motherly love originate is referred to as the moon. Thus, one can conclude that chandrama (the moon principle) is the state in which the three attributes of affection, mercifulness and motherly love are present.

c. **The Third eye :** Shankar is three-eyed, i.e. He can perceive events of the past, present and future. According to the science of Yoga the third eye means the Sushumna nadi (channel).

d. **Serpent :** One of the Names of Lord Shankar is Bhujanga-patihari. Bhujang means a serpent or pure particles, pati means the nurturer and hari means one with a garland around his neck. Bhujangapatihari thus means the One who nurtures pure particles and wears them like a garland. Various serpents represent groups of pure particles. Though externally they appear like serpents, internally they are a kind of ladder. To make spiritual progress one has to climb up holding onto the tail of the serpent. Lord Shankar adorns serpents at nine points on His body — one on the head, one around the neck, one on each arm, one on each wrist, one around the waist and one on each thigh. This implies that his body is comprised of pure particles or those serpents of pure particles play all over the body of Lord Shankar who has the universe as his form.

ARDHANARISWARA

Lord Shiva is also called Ardhanariswara. The term 'Ardhanatishvara' is a combination of three words—'ardha', 'nari' and 'ishvara', meaning respectively, 'half', 'woman' and 'Lord' or 'God', that is, Ardhanarishvara is the Lord whose half is woman. It is shiva and shakti who are inseparable. There is no existence in absence one or other. Wave-Particle duality plays a big role in modern physics and Quantum Mechanics in particular.

THE FIVE EESWARAMS — FIVE IMPORTANT SHIVA TEMPLES IN LANKA

Ishwran signifies Sivalinga. There are five Eeshwarams in Sri Lanka located in the coastal areas of the island. Long before the arrival of Vijayakumaran to Sri Lanka there was in Lanka five recognized Ishwarams of Shiva which claimed and received adoration of all India. Sri Lanka was badly affected by the Tsunami in December 2004 due to the earthquake in Indonesia. There is a history of Tsunamis that impacted the island. The legend says the story of how Viharamaha Devi, princes of Kelaniya was sent by boat by her father to prevent tsunami taking place in the western coast. Being an island and open to the sea in the south it is susceptible to Tsunamis caused by earth quakes in South East Asia, The Tsunami that hit the Western coast created many islands near Puttalam and the Jaffna peninsula. The five Ishwarams were established to protect the island from Tsunamis and other natural disasters like cyclones. They are named Naguleswaram near Keerimalai in the North, Thirukoneswaram in the fort Fredrick in Trincomalee in the east coast, Thiruketheeswaram in the West coast near Mannar, Muneeswaram near Chilaw and Dondeswaram in the Southern coast in Dondra near Tangalle. Each of these Eshwarams has a long history.

NAGULESWARAM

Naguleswaram temple is situated closer to a mineral water spring called *Keerimalai Springs* reputed for its curative properties. There is also a cave complex nearby believed to have been used for meditation by a mythical sage called Nagula Muni. Further a local myth states that an Indian Pandyan princess named *Maruthapura Veeravalli* built the nearby Mavidapuram Murugan temple after she was cured by the Keerimalai springs. After 1505 ACE it was destroyed by the Portuguese colonialists. The final destruction was recorded in 1621 ACE. The local Brahmin priests are said to have hidden the main icons before fleeing the temple. *Nagula* in Sanskrit means mongoose. *Keeri-malai* in Tamil means *Mongoose-Hill*. The legendary sage Nagula Muni, shrunk by age and austerity while meditating at a cave in Keerimalai was likened to be a mongoose that frequented the area. The sage bathed in the springs and was cured of his mongoose face. In gratitude, Nagula Muni constructed a small shrine and worshipped the Lingam enshrined there. This became known as the Thirutambaleswaram Kovil of Keerimalai and also the Naguleswaram Kovil of Keerimalai alluding to the sage. Nagulewaram is located 12 miles north of Jaffna town.

Thirukoneswaram temple of Eeswaran is located in a rock called Fort Fredrick in Trincomalee in the East coast of Sri Lanka, and has a long history. There is no evidence to prove that Raavanan built this temple. Although in the Ramayana it is said that Raavana was a strong devotee of Easwaran. The belief is that prince Vijayakumaran who landed near Puttalam in Sri Lanka from East India, with 700 friends were Hindus and there is a belief that he would have built the five Easwarams. The rock on which the temple is located is triangular in shape and hence it got its name as Thirukonamalai (Triangular shaped Mountain). When Kavaripoom pattinam, a city in Tamilnadu East which went under the sea, Thamiraparani river now flowing in Thirunelveli, was once in Lanka and got separated from Lanka. According to researchers, during this catastrophe, a triangular shaped rock must have got shifted to the East coast of Lanka. These are all assumptions. When the Pallava dynasty ruled Kancheepuram, they were good at sculpture work. Example of those sculptures are still found in Mahapalipuram. They extended their work in sculptures to Anuradhapura and Trincomalee.

Many Tamil saints such as Thirugansampantha Moorthy Nayanar, Sundaramoorthy Nayanar and Arunagiri Nayanar visited this temple and sang devotional songs. During 463 AD, a Chola prince visited Lanka and observed the demolished state of the temple. He built tanks such as Kanthalai tank around the temple and invited Vanniyar caste to do farming. The temple was maintained on the income received from farming. During 12th Century the Chola kingdom expanded in Lanka. and many Hindu temples appeared in the areas where Tamils lived. Trincomalee achieved importance and the area was managed by the Vanniyars. At one time it was the richest temple in South East Asia and many kings donated gold, pearl, diamond, coral etc to the temple.

With the arrival of Portuguese in 1505 the situation changed. In order to expand their Catholic religion, they started destroying Hindu temples. During 1624 the Portuguese General Constantine Sa, using his Portuguese soldiers, attacked and plundered the temple. The priests saved the statues by throwing them into the sea. The

Portuguese destroyed the temple, used the stones to build the fort. He informed the king of Portuguese about what was written in a stone at the entrance to the fort. It was against attacking the Portuguese. Those who plundered the temple could not enjoy the wealth. When Constantine Sa rebelled against the King, he was killed by the Portuguese soldiers. The final outcome was that the Portuguese Kingdome gradually vanished for the sins they committed against Easwaran.

The situation changed when British conquered Sri Lanka. Devotees were permitted to go to the temple and worship. Restrictions were lifted. King George's third son Fredrick became the General of the fort and the fort got the name Fort Fredrick.

In 1950, the statues and Suyambulingam that were sunk under the sea around the temple, were discovered by a photographer Mike Wilson who was involved in filming "Ranmuthuduwa" Sinhala film. This discovery brought a change in the life of Mike Wilson. He became a Hindu, started practicing meditation and became swami Kalki. There is a belief that Suyambulingam was in originally in Tibet and shifted by Raavana to his palace for worship.

DONDESWARAM. (THENAVANTHURAI)

Thondeswaram is located straight down south of Naguleswaram, near Dondra port. Both Hindus and Buddhists worship in this temple, which is located 15 miles east of Matara town. Ptolemy, a traveler (BC 150-160) visited this place and called it "Dagona", as the temple is located near a port which was once called Thvenavanthurai (Southern port). Tenavaram temple was built on vaulted arches on the promontory overlooking the Indian ocean. The central Gopuram tower of the vimana and the other Gopura towers that dominated the town were covered with plates of gilded brass, gold and copper on the roofs. Its outer body featured intricately carved domes, with elaborate arches and gates opening to various verandas and shrines of the complex, giving Tenavaram the appearance of a golden city to sailors who visited the port to trade and they relied on its light reflecting Gopura roofs for navigational purposes. This refers to the moon. Chandrasekar is also the name given to Easwaran as he has a moon on his head. In this temple the principal deity was known as "Chandra Maul Eshwaran". On the forehead of the deity was a large precious stone shaped like a moon crescent Ibunu Battuta, a Moroccan traveler, had the opportunity to visit this temple in Lanka through the Maldives. After visiting Adams peak he worshiped at the Dondeswaram temple.

The business travelers who came to southern Lanka built this temple for Easwaran and Vishnu. The central temple dedicated to Vishnu, A Perehara is celebrated annually in this temple even now. The temple was large with the roof made out of brass which shone and gave beautiful appearance for the travelers. Like Koneswaram, this temple too was destroyed by a Portuguese general De Souza d' Arronches

MUNEESWARAM — CHILAW

Muneeswaram temple is located in Chilaw, a Catholic town in the North Western province, 50 miles north from Colombo, three miles along the Chilaw Kurunegala road. The temple is located in predominantly Sinhalese area but the temple is well sponsored equally by Sinhalese, Tamils and even Catholics. The two protectors of the temple are Aiyappan and Pathirakali. Pathirakali Amman temple is located in the North of the temple. Sacrifices of animals and birds were made in this Amman temple, This ritual is now stopped after protests made by the public. Like in other Hindu temples, in 1578, the Portuguese plundered the wealth of Muneswaram temple. The river Deduru oya 142 Km in length runs North West, crossing Chilaw — Puttalam road. An Aiyappan temple is located in the river bank. Easwaran annually goes for the water cutting ceremony to this river and meets Vishnu.

THIRUKETHEESWARAM IN MANNAR

Thiruketheeswaram was a famous temple during the Chola rule in Lanka, and is located in Manthai in Mannar. In the south of Mannar, the river Malwattu oya flows into the sea. The port near the temple was once called

Manthotam. Many Arabs arrived from Arabia to do trade by selling Pearl, Elephant tusk, Silk etc. Cotton from Jaffna was exported through this port. The gulf of Mannar was once famous for pearl fishing which was promoted by the British in Arripu coastal area. On the way to Puttalam, south of Manthai an old port called Kudiramalai is located (Horse Mountain rock). Archaeological excavations have revealed that Kudiramalai was a site of ancient habitation from the 1st century BCE-to the 7th century CE. The area was once under the control of a Sera King Kattuman Koran. He was a commander in chief of the Chera Dynasty under the King Makkotai, who was an avid horseman and great patron of poetry, Korran ruled from here and administered the hilly terrain locality surrounding the ancient Tamil capital of Kudiramalai—the "Horse Mountain-Hill". During the rule of the Tamil Queen Alli Arasani (a lover of pearls) of Mannar, major changes to the western coastline occurred. According to legend, she often travelled from Kudiramalai to Mannar. She traded internationally the pearls of the Mannar seas with horses from Arabia. Several Tamils of the Mukkuvar fishing tribe migrated from Kilakarai in mainland Tamilakkam to Kudiramalai and other Malabar cities such as Puttalam and Jaffna of the Northern kingdom from the 8th century CE. Originally, Saivites fled to the west coast from mainland of Tamilnadu to escape forced conversion to Islam.

According to historical record, Vijayakumaran (543 BC-505 BC) and his 700 follower were exiled from Bengal, and landed near Thambaparni" (copper-colored palms) a river that flows through Ponparappu, a fertile area, met the Yakka queen Kuveni and married her. This history is written by a Sinhala Buddhist monk with no evidence of any record. The Sinhalese claim that they are the descendents of Viajayakumaran. Vijaykumaran after chasing away Kuveni went to Madurai and married a Tamil princess. History says that the marriage ceremony took place in Thiruketheeswaram temple. The Saivite saints Sundaramoorthy Nayanar and Thirgansambantha moorthy Nayanar sang devotional songs about Thiruketheeswaram.

*   *   *

13

The Cosmos, Sakthi in Hinduism

Cosmic dancer

In Hinduism, Shiva is considered as the cosmic dancer. According to Hindu concept Shiva performs his divine dance to destroy a weary universe and make preparations for god Brahaman to start the process of creation.The Universe is made up of matter and energy. Matter is made up of atoms and molecules (groupings of atoms) and energy causes the atoms and molecules to be always in motion—either bumping into each other or vibrating back and forth. The motion of atoms and molecules creates a form of energy called heat or thermal energy which is present in all matter. Even in the coldest voids of space, matter still has a very small but still measurable amount of heat energy.

Energy can take on many forms and can change from one form to another. Many different types of energy can be converted into heat energy. Light, electrical, mechanical, chemical, nuclear, sound and thermal energy itself can each cause a substance to heat up by increasing the speed of its molecules. So, put energy into a system and it heats up, take energy away and it cools down. For example, when we are cold, we can jump up and down and get warmer.

We know that Cosmos contains energy. The energy is generated by elementary particle called neutrino which was postulated in 1930. Neutrino a particle that has small mass and carries no charge and interacts with matter through weak nuclear force. The latest discovery of Higgs elementary particle is the "God particle" in Cosmos. Other elementary particles obtain mass by interacting with the Higgs field. Because of its possible role in producing a fundamental property of elementary particles, the Higgs boson has been referred to as the "God particle"

Pythagoras is said to have been the first philosopher to apply the term *cosmos* to the Universe. Many say that when he went to India he learned about Cosmos and Mathematics from Hindu Vedas and on his return to Greece he spoke about those subjects. The current diameter of the observable cosmos is thought to be about 93 billion light years. A light year distance is the distance traveled in a year with the speed of light. 1 light year = 9.46×10^{15} meters.

The Hindu cosmology and timeline is the closest to modern scientific timelines and even more so, which might indicate that the Big Bang is not the beginning of everything but just the start of the present cycle preceded by an infinite number of universes and to be followed by another infinite number of universes. The Rig Veda written by Hindu Rishis questions the origin of the Cosmos.

An alternate view is that the universe begins to contract after reaching its maximum expansion limits until it disappears into a fraction of a millimeter. The creation begins anew after billions of years (Solar years) of non-existence.

The term "Prakriti" means the "one that is primary". Prakriti comes before everything else. This word is a combination of the words "Pra", which means before and "Krit", which implies, to make. The Prakriti is the one pradhana – the main root, which anchors the entire universe. It is the root of all that is ever created or ever occurs in the universe. Prakriti never emerged from a cause, but it is the cause of all events taking place in this universe. Hence, while Prakriti is itself detached from and independent of everything, all is dependent on it for support. Hindu philosophy sees Prakriti and Purusha as two separate aspects of the Brahman or on or the Creative Consciousness. While Prakriti is likened to the creative energy of Mother Nature, Purusha is the consciousness that is the power of Brahman. While Prakriti gives shape to things, Purusha helps manifest them as part of the universal consciousness

The puranic view asserts that the universe is created, destroyed, and re-created in an eternally repetitive series of cycles. In Hindu cosmology, a universe endures for about 4,320,000,000 years interpreted as one day for Brahma, the creator or Kalpa and is then destroyed by fire or water elements. At this point, Brahmma rests for one night, just as long as the day. This process, named pralaya, repeats for 100 Brahma years (40 Billion Human Years) that represents Brahma's lifespan. It must be noted that Brahma is the creator but not necessarily regarded as God in Hinduism. He is mostly regarded as a creation of God.

We are currently believed to be in the 51st year of the present Brahmma and so about 156 trillion years have elapsed since he was born as Brahma. After Brahma's "death", it is necessary that another 100 Brahma years (311 Trillion, 40 Billion Years) pass until a new Brahma is born and the whole creation begins anew. This process is eternally repeated again and again.

Brahmma's day is divided in one thousand cycles (*Maha Yuga*, or the Great Year). *Maha Yuga*, during which life, including the human race appears and then disappears, has 71 divisions, each made of 14 *Manvantara* (1000) years. Each *Maha Yuga* lasts for 4,320,000 years. *Manvantara* is Manu's cycle, the one who gives birth and governs the human race.

Each *Maha Yuga* consists of a series of four shorter *yugas*, or ages. The *yugas* get progressively worse from a moral point of view as one proceeds from one *Yuga* to another. As a result, each *Yuga* is of shorter duration than the age that preceded it. The current kali Yuga (Iron Age) began in February 3102 BC in the Julian calendar.

Space and time are considered to be *maya* (illusion). What looks like 100 years in the cosmos of Brahma could be thousands of years in other worlds, millions of years in some other worlds and 311 trillion and 40 billion years for our solar system and earth. The life span of Lord Brahma, the creator, is 100 'Brahma-Years'. One day in the life of Brahma is called a Kalpa or 4.32 billion years.

Every Kalpa creates 14 Manus one after the other, who in turn manifest and regulate this world. Thus, there are fourteen generations of Manu in each Kalpa. Each Manu's life consists of 71 Each **Chaturyuga** is composed of four eras or Yugas: Satya, Treta, Dwapara and Kali. These are mainly assumptions.

The span of the **Satya Yuga** is 1,728,000 human years, **Treta Yuga** is 1,296,000 human years long, the **Dwapara Yuga** 864,000 human years and the **Kali Yuga** 432,000 human years. When Manu perishes at the end of his life, Brahamman creates the next Manu and the cycle continues until all fourteen Manus and the Universe perish by the end of Brahma's day. When 'night' falls, Brahma goes to sleep for a period of 4.32 billion years, which is a period of time equal one day (of Brahma) and the lives of fourteen Manus. The next 'morning', Brahma creates fourteen additional Manus in sequence just as he has done on the previous 'day'. The cycle goes on for 100 'divine years' at the end of which Brahma perishes and is regenerated. Brahma's entire life equals 311 trillion, 40 billion years. Once Brahma dies there is an equal period of un manifestation for 311 trillion, 40 billion years, until the next Brahma is created.

The present period is the *Kali Yuga* or last era in one of the 71 Chaturyugis (set of four Yugas/eras) in the life one of the fourteen Manus. The current Manu is said to be the seventh Manu and his name is Vaivasvat.

According to Aryabahata the Indian philosopher, the *Kali Yuga* began in 3102 BC, at the end of the *Dvapara* Yuga that was marked by the disappearance of Vishnu's Krishna avatar. Aryabhata's date is widely repeated in modern Hinduism.

Overview of Yugas:

1. **Satya Yuga (Krita Yuga):** — 1,728,000 Human years
2. **Treta Yuga:** — 1,296,000 Human years
3. **Dwapara Yuga:** — 864,000 Human years
4. **Kali Yuga:** — 432,000 Human years (5,111 years have passed; 426,889 years remain). *Kaliyuga* started in 3102 B.C.; CE 2009 corresponds to *Kaliyuga* year 5,111

It is surprising to find these figures in Indian Hindu almanacs. The almanacs also indicate the date and time of the occurrence of Solar, Lunar eclipses, whether they are partial or total and where they are visible. Hinduism speaks about eclipses and gives a different explanation for the occurrence associated with the planets.

Energies in Cosmos

In Physics and Chemistry, energy is the basis of all laws. Forces are linked with energy. Hidden energies in nature such as Electrical, Nuclear, Thermal, Chemical, Potential, Kinetic energies could be used for good and bad purposes. Nature derives its energy from cosmos. Based on the Big Bang theory, cosmos generated energy. Explosion generated the sound "Aum". Energy from nature is used for different purposes. Many years ago during Vedic period, Rishis interpreted energy in the form of Goddess Amman, Durka, Kali, Saraswathy. Lukshimi. Each of these Goddesses is linked with different actions. As per the conservation of energy there is no destruction of energy. Saraswathy the daughter of Brahman is considered as the wife of Brahamman. How can the daughter symbol of knowledge become the wife. The philosophy is that Brhamma accepted the knowledge as part of him and accept of Saraswathy not for sex.

Cosmos is in the form of an egg. This thought is in the ancient Rig Veda. The limits of the energy are the competition between expansion and contraction. There is no end for the cosmos. There is competition between attractive and repulsive forces in the stars. This stops the expansion of the cosmos. Creation and Destruction can occur at any time. In-between is the maintenance that was created. These three processes explain the actions of Brahma, Vishnu and Siva. Einstein's famous equation: $E = mc^2$, where E is energy, m is mass, and c is the speed of light in a vacuum. Mass—energy equivalence does not imply that mass may be "converted" to energy, but it allows for *matter* to be converted to energy. Through all such conversions, *mass* remains conserved, since it is a property of matter and any type of energy. In physics, mass must be differentiated from matter.

The estimate of the age of Universe is 13.72 ± 0.12 billion years. Brahmma, the creator, is the consort of Saraswathy [knowledge] and together, they represent the creative force. After we obtain Knowledge, we can do anything. Knowledge takes us up to the highest level of consciousness known as Bramhaloka. Knowledge is the remover of fear and leads to awareness, enlightenment and confidence in life. Goddess Saraswathy governs ten objects of transcendent knowledge.

Laximi is the Goddess of light and the representation of universal energy. Out of one of her hands, money flows. This shows that she represents CASH FLOW and controls the wealth from business ventures and investment prospects. MONEY is really one form of the universal energy. In the earnings cycle, you go to work; there you expend your energy that was derived from the absorption of your food, which in turn will be converted into Labor for which the money you receive will be the measure. When this energy is not earned properly and not spent in a thoughtful and respectful manner, then the energy becomes destructive. MONEY is really light energy.

Swami Ram Charran shows how Hindu Gods are really the periodic Table of elements that keeps all of us alive. He shows how Einstein derived his famous equation $E=mc^2$ from the Hindu texts, how Newton knew about the colours of the Sun from the Hindu God Surya, and how the nine forms of electro-magnetic energy since creation was known as the nine forms of Laximi, the Hindu Goddess of Light. Newton said that white light consists of seven colors. Long before he made that discovery the Sun god is represented by an idol driving seven horses representing the seven colors and this could be seen in Konrak temple for the sun.

Durka represents braveness. It is another form of energy. Durka uses this form of energy to overcome evils. There are puranic stories explaining the braveness of Durka.

EXPLANATION OF THE ENERGY DIAGRAM.

In the diagram it is important to note the direction of the arrows and the links. The needs are there for Man, Religion, and Science. To meet his needs, man approaches the energy in different forms. Politics exists in all three areas. In Religion and Science if knowledge is used for bad purpose, energy is wasted. A typical example is the use of the Atom bomb (Nuclear Energy) during the second world war which killed thousands of people and polluted the environment. Economy, and wealth are in all three. Man uses meditation to concentrate mind energy, expands his knowledge and unties the secrets of nature. Man attempts to know all about energy. but that is not complete. Man shares the energy with Religion and nature. In Hinduism, energy is interlocked with nature. We have seen importance given for trees in temples and worshiped. The use of Pancha Boothas (Five sources of Energies namely Water — Air — Fire — Space — Earth are used in rituals). There are five temples in India to signify each of the five boothas. Uses of animals as vehicles by deities are all Energy transformation. Among animals, the cow and bull are considered as sacred animals. Pictures from the Indus Valley civilization prove the importance of the bull. The main reason may be that people used bulls for cultivation and transport.

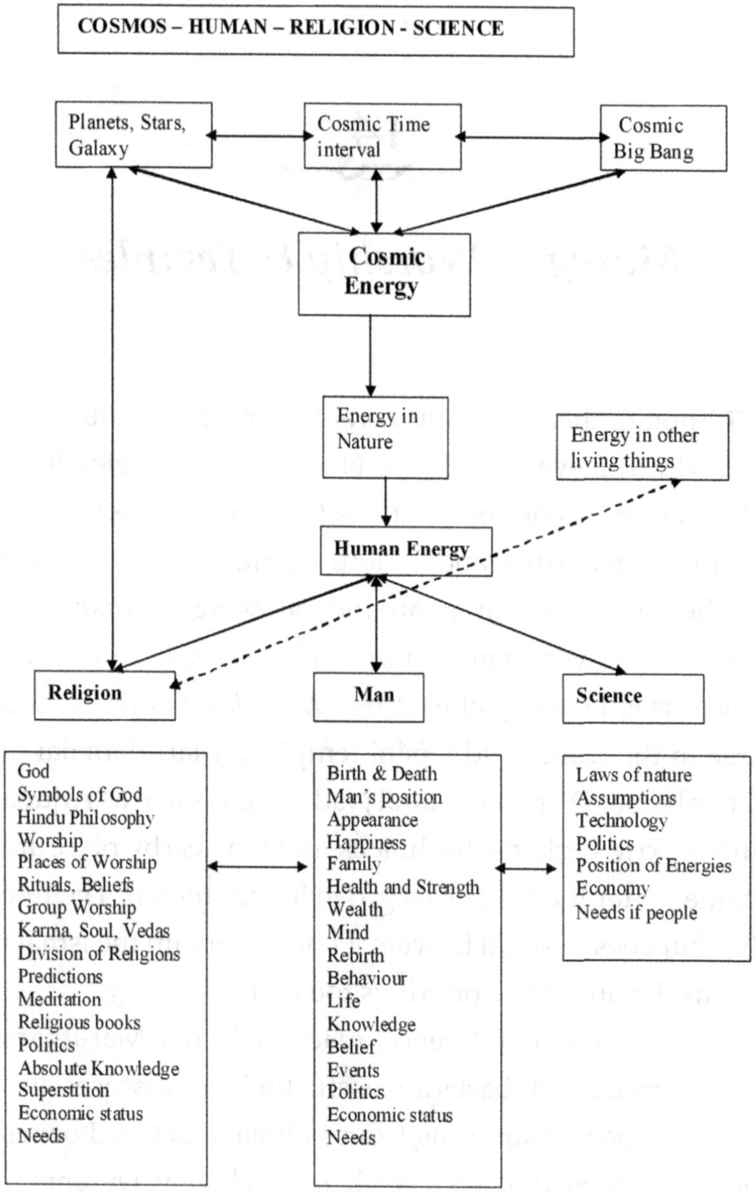
COSMOS – HUMAN – RELIGION - SCIENCE
Planets, Stars, Galaxy
Cosmic Time interval
Cosmic Big Bang
Cosmic Energy
Energy in Nature
Energy in other living things
Human Energy
Religion
Man
Science
God
Symbols of God
Hindu Philosophy
Worship
Places of Worship
Rituals, Beliefs
Group Worship
Karma, Soul, Vedas
Division of Religions
Predictions
Meditation
Religious books
Politics
Absolute Knowledge
Superstition
Economic status
Needs
Birth & Death
Man's position
Appearance
Happiness
Family
Health and Strength
Wealth
Mind
Rebirth
Behaviour
Life
Knowledge
Belief
Events
Politics
Economic status
Needs
Laws of nature
Assumptions
Technology
Politics
Position of Energies
Economy
Needs if people

14

Murugan Worship & Temples

Though there are innumerable temples for Murugan (Karthigeyan) in Tamil Nadu, some temples have different types of Temple trees (thala vrikushas). Apart from the mango tree and the lotus plant, the trees attached to the Murugan temples are the following: *Marudham* or Queen's Flower *Panneer or Indian Lavender, Punnai, Nelli, Mahizham, Pala or Jak) fruit tree. Marudham* is the sacred tree in the Dandayudhapani temple at Marudamalai in Coimbatore District in Tamil Nadu. It is known as Arjuna in Sanskrit. Perhaps this hillock and the nearby place are named after the *marudham* grove in that region. The tree has bunches of small flowers. People worship the isthala viriuksha and make offerings too god.

There are lot of references made to the tree Marutham in Ayurveda as its barks are useful for heart diseases. It is good for people suffering from asthma. Fractured bones get strengthened when it is taken with honey. Dysentery is stopped by taking the decoction of the bark powder of

Marudham. Young ladies who fear pimples, its paste is a good medicine. Even the sting of scorpion is cured when its ashes are applied on the place of the bite. As it is an anti-microbial agent, it purifies the environment.

Panner is very sacred to Murugan in Tiruchendur as the sacred ash (*vibhudhi*) prasadam is given to the devotees by the temple priests only in the panneer leaves. The white flowers are small in shape with a lovely fragrance. *Pannee*r tree is sacred to Siva and Vishnu in some temples. As it blooms at night, the whole surroundings are well scented. It used for archana and in garlands to deities. This tree has some medicinal effects too. The wood of the tree is used to stop dysentery as well as to make nice furniture. The pustular swelling of the children is cured when the paste of the panneer leaves are applied.

Though *punnai* flowers are very closely associated with Siva as one of the eight flowers offered to Him during morning offerings, the punnai tree is the isthala viriuksha of Murugan in the form of Subramaniaswami in Peacock in Cuddalore district. It is an indigenous tree and its blooming denotes prosperity. There are many references in *puranas* to *Punnaga vanam* (the forest of *punnai* tree). It has been a practice in villages in ancient times if the tree failed to bloom in time, the local women would dance around the barren *punnai* tree and kick the same at the bottom of the tree and surprisingly it would start blooming. Punnai flower juice cures venereal diseases and boils. Nervous disorders could be treated with its flowers. The powder made out of the *punnai* leaves is good for getting relief for giddiness and head ache. The juice taken from its bark is useful to stop internal and external bleeding. It is surprising to note that the intra-muscular injection of the oil taken out of *punnai* seeds reduces the pain in leprosy. Though this green colour oil does not have good odour, it reduces and cures pain in joints, muscles, ulcers and skin diseases. The *punnai* fruits give a gum.

Mahizham is the i*sthala viriksha* for Siva, Vishnu and Murugan and sacred not only to the Saivites and Vaishnavites but to Jains and Buddhists too. Mahizhzm trees find their place in the Amaravati and Sanchi stupas. It is an emblem of Neminatha, a Jain Tirthankara and he attained enlightenment under this tree. It is the temple tree of Sri Kandaswamy temple at Tirupporur in Kanchipuram District and Sri Kulandaivel temple in Madurai District. This tree has small but very sweet smelling flowers. Even if it dries, the smell remains. There are many myths associated with this tree. It is believed that the tree blooms if women eat under its shade or beautiful women spits on it. In Indian society, it is a boon to get a male child. It is believed that the women who do not have male children beget a male child if they tie a small cradle to the tree after going round the temple. Similarly, people tie threads to the branches of the sacred tree if they want their wishes to be fulfilled. They untie the thread after the fulfilment of their wishes.

Pala is one of the three important fruits, the other two being plantain and mango. In Kollimalai in Salem District is famous for the Murugan temple. The sacred tree of the temple is *Jack*. It is not known to many that the leaves of Jack are as auspicious as banana leaves. It is interesting to note that this tree that jack fruit is depicted in the early Buddhist sculptures. The shade of this tree is so sacred that all Gods, Agamas, Sasthiras and Vedas are said to have gathered under its shade. It is believed if one waters this sacred tree with one pitcher of water, it is equal to have performed *abisheka (special puja using milk)* to all the gods.

Hinduism has often been coined as an "environmental friendly" religion. Hindus regard everything around them as pervaded by a subtle divine presence, may it be rivers, mountains, lakes, animals, flora, fauna, the mineral world, as well as the stars and planets. It is so because the Divine reality is present as Prana/Shakti energy, power, in every electron, particle, atom, and cell and in every manifestation of matter. It is its very fabric. Just like the sparks of a fire are of the same essence as the fire they come from, so is the entire creation, of the same essence as the Divine. Just as Hindus greet each other saying "Namaste", which means: I recognize and salute the Divine within you, so do they recognize the same Divine essence, in all around them.

Mountains play an important part in Hinduism. Thiruvannamalai, Palani, Marudhamalai, Thirukalukuntram are some of the mountains in Tamil Nadu where Hindu Gods in temples are located. Many mountains consist of minerals and generate vibration from crystals. Herbal trees are in abundance in the mountain in Palani and around 3000 B.C, when the world was waking up to evolution, it witnessed the presence of Siddhar Bogar, a powerful astrologer, and a yogi who had mastered the science of medicine perfectly. Bhogar was an expert in siddha medicine and it is said that according to the last wishes of his guru, Bhogar proceeded to China to spread the knowledge of siddha sciences. His journey is said to have been made with the aid of an aircraft; he demonstrated to the Chinese the details of the construction of the aircraft and later built for them a sea-going craft using a steam engine.

Ganga, Jamuna. Narmada, Indus, Kaveri Rivers are well respected by Hinduism but people does not care and pollute the river. The ashramams are built by the side of the river and Rishis take a bath in the morning before starting meditating. The river water flows through the medicinal herbs in the mountain range of Himalayas, act as disinfectant. The River Ganges or Ganga is perhaps the holiest river in any religion. Besides being a sacred river, Ganga is also worshiped as a deity in Hinduism; Ganga water is used in various religious ceremonies of the Hindus. Even Science has proved that Ganga water is pure and bacteria free. Ganga water can be kept for years without any problem. In the banks of the Sarasvati River, Vedas flourished during Vedic period and its name is mentioned 72 times in the Rigveda, appearing in all books except for book four. Between 6000 and 4000 B.C., the Saraswati flowed as a great river and it disappeared in the course of time due to climatic changes. Rivers constitute the lifeline of any country and some of the world's great civilizations (Indus Valley, Mesopotamian, and Egyptian) have all prospered on banks of river systems. Hindus consider rivers as sacred and have personified them as deities and sung their praises in their religious literature, In *Vedas*, river Saraswati, during its heydays, is described to be much bigger than Sindhu or the Indus River.

Among the various Hindu deities, Karthigeyan is worshiped mainly by the Tamil community in countries like Tamilnadu, Sri Lanka, Singapore, Malaysia, Re Union. With the migration of Tamils to the western world many Murugan temples have originated in the name of Murugan temples such as Nallur, Selvasanathi, Kathirgamam, and Thiruchendur to cater to the people from those areas.

God Murugan's name means beauty and He is considered as a Dravidian God. People say that Murugan worship started from the time of the Gupta period in North India. The origin of worshipping Murugan is similar to Worship of Hermes by Asyrians. This is similar to the worshiping of Ra (the Sun) by the Egyptians.

LAND DIVISION AND WORSHIP

Idol worship in Tamilnadu is based on the division of land and the work done by the people from that area. Four of the geographical regions are described as landscapes that occur naturally in the Tamil areas. These are: Kurinji — mountainous regions, associated with union, Mullai — forests, associated with waiting, Marutham — cropland, associated with quarreling, and Neythal — seashore, associated with pining. The fifth — Paālai or desert, associated with separation — They were described in the Tolkappiyam, a work on the grammar of Tamil language as being naturally existing landscapes. Murugan is worshiped by hunters who hunt using spears (Vel), bow and arrows in mountainous areas. It is the means to supply food as energy for their life. Hence Murugan temples are mainly found on the top of rocks such as Palani, Marutamalai and Viralimalai

The vehicle for Murugan is the peacock. Murugan is also called Alagan (Beauty) and note that Peacock is a beautiful bird. Ganapathy, the eldest brother of Murugan played an important part in the love affair of Valli (Veddah girl) and Karthigeyan. The story centers on a farming village Kathirgamam in a jungle in southern Lanka. A historical temple of Kathirgmam exists in that village, respected by Hindus, Muslims and Buddhists. The river Manickka Ganga flows through that village. As Valli was a Veddah girl (Hunter's daughter), puja is done in a typical Sinhalese style with Sinhalese damsels dressed like Veddah girls, serving Prasadam. Kapuralas who do the pujas are believed to be descended from indigenous Veddah people. The mouth of the priest is tied with a white cloth and puja carried out and only he is permitted to enter the inner sanctum where a holy Yantra is kept. Devotees believe that a strong Yantra exists in the heart of the temple, and once in a way it is taken out in a box on procession on the back of an Elephant.

According to legend, Karthigeyan, the second son of Siva and Parvathy has two wives, namely Deivayani, with North Indian Ariyan connection and Valli with the Dravidian link. Deivayani represents spirituality and Valli the love within the soul.

Devotees of Murugan while climbing the rock carry Kavadi (Carrying stick). Some devotees pierce their cheeks with sharp spears. They shave the head symbolizing the incident that took place between Karthigeyan and his father Shiva over a Mango fruit. In anger Karthigeyan shaved his head because he lost the contest with Ganesh and went and meditated with only a loin cloth to hide his genitals.

Kathirgamam temple

KATHIRGAMAM (A VILLAGE WHERE SITHARS LIVED)

The temple for Murugan in Kathirgamam is located 228 Km south east of Colombo. "Gamam" means in Tamil farming village area. Paddy means Kathir. Hence Kathirgamam means a village where paddy is grown. The village is located in Yala wild life in sanctuary in southern Sri Lanka. The area was once occupied by elephants and wild animals. A river named Maanika Ganga flows through this village. From 1972, devotees started walking more than 400 miles from Northern Lanka, along the eastern coastal area via Trincomalee, Batticaloa, and Pothuvil to Kathirgamam. According to Sinhalese, historians, Kathirgamam temple was constructed 1st century BC by King Dutugemunu. Dutugemunu was the son of Viharamahdevei, wife, of Kavantissa. She ruled Kirinda an area near the Yala games sanctuary. Before going to war with the Tamil Chola king Ellalan in Anuradhapura, Dutugemunu meditated in the bank of the river Maanika Ganga, prayed for help from Murugan and went to the battle. When he won the war, he became a strong devotee of Murugan. This is a legendary story narrated by the Singhalese. There are several curtains that hang in the moolasthanam (main shrine) to hide the Yantra and the priest who does the puja is called Kapurala.

There are many interesting stories that happened in Kathirgamam, which prove the greatness and purity of the temple. During 203 AD, Babaji Nadaraj born in south India, at the age of eleven went to Kathirgamam in search of his guru Boganathar sithar. Under a banyan tree Babaji meditated for six months. At the start he meditated for 24 hours and later he reached a level of meditating continuously for 48 days. The banyan tree under which the Babaji meditated was cut down by a person, he became mad and committed suicide. There is a small black stone statue on the outside the main Kathirgamam temple of this deathless Saint Babaji who introduced Kriya Yoga to humanity as well as Devayanai worship and a temple for her exist there now.

Kalyangiri Swami was responsible for Kathirgamam to become popular in India, during 16th century, He was called Muthulinga swamigal in Lanka. After Kalyanagiri swamigal," Paalkudi baba" became popular. He was a Brahmin from Allahabad. Since he had the habit of drinking milk very often, he got the name Palkudi baba.

A king without children, prayed at Kathirgamam, promising that if a child is born, he will donate the child to the temple. A beautiful daughter was born and the king named her Balasundari. The king took the daughter to Kathirgamam and left her there to serve God. She became a nun for the temple. The Kandyan king Rajasinghe came to know about the beauty of Balasundari and send a request for her to marry him. She refused the king's request to marry him. He ordered few of his soldiers to go to Kathirgamam, arrest and bring her by force to him. Balasundari prayed to God Murugan to save her. God fulfilled her request. At that time British forces invaded the Kandyan kingdom, arrested the king and took him as prisoner to Velore in Tamil Nadu. The king ultimately died in Velore. She lived until she became old and after her assistant Mangalpuri swamigal lived in Kathirgamam. There is a memorial for her in the temple.

During the British rule, an administrative officer who worked as Justice of peace in the Badulla Kachchcri, suffered from a serious illness. He was worried that he did not get any promotion because of his illness. His sickness could not be cured. He prayed to God Kathirgamam and went to the temple. He met Paalkudi Baba and prayed explaining his sickness. While one day when he was talking with the devotees about the greatness of Kathirgamam God, a madman met him, and said "when you return to Badulla Kachcheri, you will get a transfer order to go to North. As per the mad man's prediction he was transferred to the Northern Province, where he met an Ayurvedic physician and had treatment. His sickness was cured and became strong devotee of God Kathirgamam.

In my experience in Kahirgaman, when I went with my parents, sister and brother during 1950's to fulfill a vow, the temple was crowded and there was no place to keep our baggages and sleep. We were tired after travelling 350 miles from Puttalam, by Train, Bus and finally by cart and had no place to sleep. My father was a Murugan devotee as our house in Jaffna was closer to the Nallur Murugan temple. He prayed to Murugan of Kathirgamam." He cried saying "Muruga, I have come to see you from a long distance with my family. Please do not leave my family alone. At that time an old man with holy ash and sandal wood pottu in his forehead, approached my father and said "Ayah. Do you want a place to keep your things and rest? Come with me I will show you a room. You will be safe there" My father could not believe it. The old man disappeared after few minutes after getting him a room to rest. My father searched for him to thank him but could not meet him. He thought that it was Kathirgama Murugan who helped him.

Long ago there was sanctity in the temple. Devotees crossed the Manicka Ganga (river) on a hanging bridge. There were no big hotels. Ramakrishna mission provided resting place and free food for devotees. Many business men from south, provided rice and vegetables free of cost to the Mission. But political leadership upset the free service provided by the mission. Hotels were constructed. In due course, Liqueor and Non vegetarian food were served. In 50's, devotees walked 11 miles and also went by cart from Tissamaharagama, a village west of Kathiragamam. Hoppers and banana were served to devotees by the villagers. But things changed and bus service is now available up to the door steps. It is the respect and love for him that is required by Kathirgama Murugan. Many Sithars (Yogis) and great men lived, meditated and attained Samadhi. Great vibrational energy exits in that environment.

Sella Kathirgammam is a place where Ganesh temple is located 3 miles northwest of Kathirgammam by the side of a stream. As per the legendary story Ganesh was instrumental for the Murugan Valli love affair and it is this place where Valli met the elephant when Murugan was courting Valli, Kumbuk trees provide the shade for the devotees.

Nallur Kandasamy Temple

Nallur Kandasamy temple is located two miles from Jaffna town and has a long history and incidents. It is a popular rich temple and patronized by large number of devotees. Historians are of the view Ukirasingan when ruling fell in love with the princes Maaruthapiravalli who came to Keerimalai on pilgrimage from Tamil Nadu. He built a Murugan temple in Mavidapuram as per her request. He changed his capital from Kadiramalai to Singainagar. One time a place called Nallur in Poonahiri was the capital. Some historians are of the view the first Nallur Kandasamy temple was built in Nallur Poonahari, a place between Paranthan and Poonahari. The name Nallur means a good town and it got its name from a village in Tamilnadu. On the orders of Selvarayan's son Pandi Malavan, Pandyans appointed a King for Jaffna and Prince Singai Aryan arrived in Jaffna in 1200 AD. He founded the Arya Chakravarthi dynasty, which lasted 403 years. The prince Singai Arian came with religious priests to the Jaffna Kingdom and established a kingdom for himself with high walls, administrative set up, judiciary, army barracks and place for horses and elephants to be trained. He was called Koolankai Singaiarian. He made an educated Brahimin Buvanekubahu as the chief minister for the Kingdom. First in remembrance of the Sivan temple he worshiped in Madurai, he built the Kailasanathar Sivan temple in Nallur. As per the book Kailasmaalai, the temple was built in 870 AD Buvanekabahu. There is confusion in that date whether it is 948 or 1248 AD. There is nothing wrong in saying that Buvanekubahu built the temple during 948 AD in a place called Muthirai Santhai, on Point Pedro road, closer to the existing temple. The location was called "Kurrukal valavu" (Land of the chief priest). The temple continued to be popular until 13nth century.

Buvaneku bahu was the name given to Senpaga Perumal, a Kerala prince from Panicker caste. Panickers are teachers of a martial Kalari art in Kerala. He was the adopted son of Parakiramabahu the 6th king who ruled Kotte. Senpaga Perumal being a good warrior and Brahmin, served the King as a mercenary. The King started looking him after and adopted him as his son. Senpaga Perumal was sent to capture Nallur, and he destroyed the temple and land at Kurukkal valavu. To avoid getting a bad name from people he reconstructed the temple in the same place and ruled the area by the name of Sri Sangabothi Buvanekabahu. Even today his name is honoured in the prayers said in the temple.

During 1478 Kanagasuriyan and then his first son Singai Pararajasekeran ruled the place. To get protection from God, he established temples around the Nallur kingdom. To mention, in the west he built the powerful and popular Veera Maha Kali Amman temple worshiped by Sangili king. Sangili fought with the Portuguese in the vicinity of the Veeramaha Kali Amman temple. In the North Satanathar Sivan temple, In the East Viyilil Ularntha Pillayar temple exposed to sun light and in the west Kailasapillayar temple.

Before the Murugan temple was built in the present place there was a Muslim Yogi and a Fakir by the name of Sikandar who was respected by people of all religions. He guided and fought with Tamil soldiers when Portuguese attempted to destroy the Murugan temple. He died in the war. A vel was planted in the place where he died and people trust a tomb is there inside the present Murugan temple in the place he was buried. There is separate access for the Muslims to this tomb. Muslims are permitted to sell camphor and things for Puja and have access to the tomb of the Fakir.

One time in Tamilnadu, the Tamils who were converted to Hinduism, because of the invasion of Muslims in Tamil nadu, called themselves as the Kantahsaibu group and migrated to Kodikamam in Jaffna Peninsula and to places such as Usan, Mirusivil and Eluthumattuval to do business. The name Usan (Husain) signifies that it was a Muslim area once. Because they could not do business successfully in those areas, they moved to the present Nallur temple area and built a mosque.

In 1620, like other Hindu temples, the Portuguese after cunningly defeating king Sangili, destroyed the Murugan temple to the ground. They built a Catholic church in the place where there was the Murugan temple. In 1658 the Dutch captured Jaffna from the Portuguese. They introduced protestant religion in Jaffna. They destroyed the Catholic Church and built a Church of their religion. During 1734 a small temple was built in the land near Yamunari. They established a Vel and worshiped it. A person by the name Don Juan Ragunatha Maapana Mudaliyar, used his influence with Dutch administration and got legal permission to build the temple in the present location. Krisnayar Suppiar was of assistance to Ragunatha Mudaliyar to build the temple. When he saw the Muslims getting settled in that area, he tried to buy the land from them but failed. As a protest they polluted the wells used by Muslims by dropping the meat of pigs. The Muslims had no other alternative but to sign a contract in that area. to move out from Naavanthurai to Sonaga Theru and established their businesses. Many Muslims live there They gave permission for Muslims who wanted to worship through a door in the west of the temple. In 1773 Aruumuga Navalar wanted to replace the Vel and build the temple using black stones but that was not agreed upon. Moreover sacrificing a goat and applying its blood to the wheels of the cart during car festival was to be stopped. This action was taken to ensure that when the cart moves in the crowd no one gets killed as such it is done as a sacrifice to prevent any accidents happening during the car festival. Now during

Poongavanam festival, Venison is served in Prasadam. This is done in Kathirgama as well. He also filed a case on the temple to show the accounts and won the case in his favour. The location where cart is parked is called "Theradi", was popular because Yogar Swami and Kadai swami meditated at Theradi.

Maviddapuram temple, many years ago was a small place of worship. According to legend, the temple was built by the Chola princess, Maruthapura Veeravalli, who had been cured of her ailments and her horse-like face had disappeared after bathing in the Keerimalai tank. It is at this kovil that the chariot stands to this day retaining much of its former splendour. The Chola Princess Maruthapuravalli from Tamil nadu was cursed and to cure her curse travelled to Kerimalai and prayed for healing. The water of Keerimalai had curable properties. The king Ukiramasingan when he saw her fell in love with her beauty, wanted to marry her and kidnapped her by force. On her request he completed Kanthavel Murugan temple. The king got down the statues through Kankesanthurai for the temple and that is how the port got its name as Kankesan referring to Murugan. During 785 AD the temple was established. The title Ma in Tamil refers to horse. Since Maruthapuravalli's face appeared like a horse and was cured, the temple got its name as Maviddapuram. The temple festival starts one week before Nallur Kandasamy Kovil festival and ends on Adi Amaavasai with the water cutting ceremony. Five carts are used in the car festival. The temple is highly orthodox and owned by high caste Brahmins and low caste people were not permitted to enter the temple. The area was inhabited by educated people and the place is called Tellipalai.

It is believed that god Shanmuga performs a secret dance on the fifth day of the Annual festival and thousands of people gather to witness this unusual and appealing sight. The climax of this festival which falls on the last day, the 25th day, is the water cutting ceremony or the well-known Adi Amavasai Theertham at Keerimalai in the waters of the Palk Strait, ever famous for its curative purposes. in May of 1872, a son Yogar was born to Ambalavanar and Sinnachi Amma not far from the Kandaswamy temple in Maviddapuram. He became a yogi and is respected by many.

A dent appeared in the management of the temple owned by an orthodox Brahimin priest when low caste people from that area demanded entry into the temple with the help of Peking communist party. It started in 1968 as a non violent request but turned into a violent political issue. Educated people like professors were against the temple entry. Many said that a temple is a place for worship for all categories of people. The temple owner, a Brahimin was insisted that cleanness and purity of the temple should ne maintained as low caste people were not permitted to the temple. The temple high priest wanted to control the temple so that no one could ask for the temple accounts. It should be noted that Murugan is the God of the hunters, who could also be considered as low caste people who hunt and eat meat and fruits. The explanation given by the chief priest was contradictory.

www.mathagal.com

Selvasannathi Temple

The other popular Murugan temple in the Jaffna peninsula is Selvasanathi temple near Thondamanaru River. This temple is well patronized by the Vadamaratchi population. Since travel to Kathirgamam took a long time, they called this temple as a duplicate and named it Sella Kathirgamam. Traders used Point Pedro, Valvettiturai ports for trade, so they worshiped Murugan and gave of their wealth to the temple. The method of puja here is similar to Kathirgamam as the priest ties his mouth with a cloth during the puja. This may be for avoiding pollution or following the tradition. There are 18 resting places called madams in the temple. Yogis have meditated under the tree and the area attained sanctity. Karunakara Thondaman was sent to Vadamaratchi to procure salt supplies by Kulathunga

Cholan, who reigned in Chola Nadu. The temple by the side of the newly cut waterway was the place of worship of the settlement that was found in the locality. In order to transport salt from Navatkuli to the port, to export to Tamil Nadu, Thondaman deepened the canal and named it Thondaman river.

MURUGAN TEMPLES IN EASTERN PROVINCE

Many parts of the Eastern province have thick forests and Veddah's lived in these forests. They lived in places like Thambuvilla and Thirikovil. Eastern Sri Lanka is a region where various ethnic groups, including the tribal Veddas, have long been living together. Tamil speaking Hindus are the majority group in Batticaloa; their social formation is based on a rigid *kuti* (matrilineal clan) system. This region is known for Kannagai (Pathini) Mother Cult practice in this region varies from ancient patterns to modern types. Although Batticaloa district in Eastern Sri Lanka is rich in ritual traditions, few studies have been carried out in this regard. This study analyses these Skanda-Murugan traditions in a socio-anthropological perspective. The Skanda temples of Mantur, Ukantai, Tanta malai, and Chittanti were based on the legendary story that God Skanda after successfully defeating the Asuras was returning east, when he encountered the Vākūra Hills. The God in his anger split the hill into two with his Vēl. Three bright rays emanated from this, and each one of the range traveled in different directions. One of these reached Mantūr and sheltered within the tillai trees, which came to be patronized by the Veddahs.

During the Chola period, Queen Cīrpātatēvi left for the northern kingdom (Cinka Nakar), but before leaving handed over her golden vēl to Cīrpata family members, she requested them to cherish it. To this day, members of this group are given prominence at all temple functions.

The origin of the temple is centered on the Veddahs, who for their protection and safety used their weapons the bow and arrow as symbols of worship.

Another myth relates to the might of God Skanda-Murugan. A detachment of Portuguese soldiers after the conquest of the East advanced toward the temple to loot it, but they were attacked by wasps. The frightened soldiers fled for their lives, leaving behind their weapons, including muskets and swords. The latter are still kept in the sanctum sanctorum as reminders of the power of the God residing at Mantūr.

A permanent temple was built in 1215-1248 by King Nāka., and its structure is a replica of the temple in Kathirkāmam. In the outer courtyard there are two smaller temples. One of these is for Theyvayānai Amman and the other for Valli Amman. In the inner courtyard there are two shrine rooms: one for Pillaiyār and the other for Nākatampiran. There is a worshipping platform for Kumāra Tampiran. In addition there are nine stone pillars as, each one representing Valli's brother and the other eight the Attatikku Pālakar, meaning those in charge of protection of the eight directions.

Patterns of worship at Mantūr are ancient and virtually identical to those in Kathirkāmam. The officiating priest is called Kappukanār, equivalent of Kappurāla in Katirkāmam. The priest is chosen from the Cīrpata kulam (clan). The Veddahs is also given equal importance; for instance, the Ārāti Pen or the woman performing the lamp rituals, is chosen from the Veddah group.

Ukantai Murugan temple is at the foot of the Ukantai Malai, a remote rock-hill on the coast at the intersection of the Eastern and Southern Provinces. Here the Murugan temple is at the foot of the hill, while his sweetheart Valli occupies the peak. This is another place where King Rāvana is said to have rested and worshipped on his way to Konesvaram in Trincomalee. The theme of taking rest is reflected in the name Ukantai, for it is said that here Lord Murugan and others 'sat down' (utkantār) and rested.

According to another myth, the third ray from Vākura Hill reached here and came to rest on this hilltop, making it a favorite site for Murugan worship. There is yet a third myth according to which, Valli and Murugan arrived in separate stone boats (which still rest on the beach) to reside on top of the Ukantai Malai. The temple is located along the eastern shores of the country, along which the pilgrims walk to Kathirkāmam. In places like Panama and Kumana, which are close to Ukantai, Tamils and Sinhalese lived in harmony even down to the present day.

The devotees offer as in other temples cooked food, fruits etc. Some of them prepare milk rice and sweet meats in the outer courtyard. At present soldiers as well as local villagers offer live poultry to the deity requesting His protection.

*　*　*

15

Vishnu Worship

HINDU DEITIES WORSHIPED BY SINHALESE COMMUNITY

In Hinduism, Buddha is viewed as an Avatar of Vishnu Hindu texts including Bhagavata Purana, enlist Buddha as an Avatar of Vishnu. In the Puranic text Bhagavata Purana, he is the twenty-fourth of twenty-five avatars, prefiguring a forthcoming final incarnation. Similarly, a number of Hindu traditions portray Buddha as the most recent (ninth) of ten principal avatars. This is one of the main reasons that in Buddhist Viharas in Lanka, Vishnu idol too is worshiped along with the Buddha statue. The Idol of Ganesh is also worshiped by Sinhala Buddhsits along with Karthigeyan. Many Singhala farmers in Lanka, consider Ganesh as a protector of farming, hence Ganesh temples are constructed for him in the farming areas and due respect given to him by boiling rice with milk. The other deity worshiped by Sinhalese is Pathini Goddess, called Kannagi Amman.

This worship was imported from Kerala (Sera kingdom) by King Gajabahu through Jambukola (Mathagal) port in the North and worshiped in the Kandy Perahara with reverence. Sinhalese consider her as protector of chastity and infectious diseases. The Sinhala Buddhists believe that the Pattini is a guardian deity of Buddhism. Many Kannagi temples are constructed in Sinhalese areas mainly eastern province, and the details are given in the section on Kannagi Amman worship.

What that is created will have to be maintained before destruction. Once it completes it life time it will be destroyed. This is the law of nature. These three functions are the basis in Hinduism and refer it to Brahamma, Vishnu and Linga. In science these functions are vital. The laws are related to these functions. In the Cosmos, centripetal forces move toward a point for the cosmos to exist and to preserve the Cosmos. This refers to Vishnu. It is the Centrifugal force that moves out that causes destruction.

Vishnu is regarded as a major God in Hinduism and Indian mythology. He is considered as the preserver of the universe while two other major Hindu Gods Brahma and Shivalinga are regarded respectively, as the creator and destroyer of the universe.

The original worship of Vishnu, by the Aryan conquerors of India or the original Dravidian inhabitants is not definitely known. It is throughout that this literature and especially through incarnations that Vishnu is raised to higher rankings within the Hindu pantheon. He becomes the prominent second God of the Tirimurthi, the Hindu Triad, while Brahma is first and Shiva is third.

In some Puranic literature Vishnu is said to be eternal, an all-pervading spirit, and associated with the primeval waters that are believed to have been omnipresent before the creation of the universe.

The concept of Vishnu being the preserver of the world came relatively late in Hinduism. Presumably it sprang from two other beliefs: that men attain salvation by faithfully following predetermined paths of duty, and that powers of good and evil (Gods and Demons) are in contention for domination over the world. When these powers are upset, it is further believed that Vishnu descends to earth, or his avatar, to equalize the powers. Further it is thought that ten such incarnations or reincarnations of Vishnu will occur. Nine descents are said to have already occurred, the tenth is yet to come. Rama and Krishna were the seventh and eighth.

Another interesting speculation concerning Vishnu's role as preserver among many modern scholars is that it is characteristic of the practitioners of Hinduism to raise local legendary heroes to Gods in the Hindu pantheon.

Vishnu is portrayed as blue or black skinned and has four arms. He has a thousand names and their repetition is an act of devotion. The way the Linga worshipers apply three stripes of holy ash horizontal in the forehead, Vishnu worshiper apply Namam. Vibhuti expresses the concept that this world we live in and the universe are driven by the functions of creation, preservation and destruction as enacted by the Triad.

Namam consists of three vertical lines joined at the base, the two outer white lines signifying the worship of Brahamma and Vishnu and the red centre line signifying the worship Mahalakshmi. The Namam (Thirunamam) signifies the fact the men and women of this world will all be transformed. In Hindu temples red and white stripes signify the temple and the explanation is that the two colours namely white signifies male energy (Sivam) and Red the female energy the Sakthi. These symbols identify whether the person who has those symbols in the forehead is Saivaite or Vaishanvite. This division exists predominantly among Hindus. The rituals are different.

The ten incarnations or 'Dasa Avatara' of Lord Vishnu is an extraordinary recording of the evolution of human Life, Lord Vishnu descends on Earth to uphold dharma and to cleanse the earth of evil. So far, Lord Vishnu has appeared nine times on earth and the tenth, Kalki, is expected. The sequence of appearance of Lord Vishnu on earth is in tune with the evolutionary theory. In fact, the ten incarnations of Lord Vishnu is an amazing recording of the advancement of human civilization. All this was recorded by Hindu sages thousands of years before Christ.

The first incarnation or avatar of Lord Vishnu was in the form of a fish and is known as 'Matsya Avatar.' It has now been confirmed by Science through various experiments that the first life forms evolved underwater. The second incarnation of Lord Vishnu was in the form of a tortoise known as 'Kurma Avatar.' Tortoise is an amphibious creature capable of living both on land and in water and it indicates the moving of life form from underwater to surface of Earth. The fourth incarnation of Lord Vishnu is the half-man half-animal form known as 'Narasimha Avatar.' This incarnation starts the transformation from animal to human form. The fifth incarnation of Lord Vishnu is the dwarf or pigmy sized human being known as the 'Vamana avatar.' The transition from the beast form to the human form results in the development of intelligence. The sixth incarnation of Lord Vishnu is the forest dweller known as 'Parasuram.' He has developed weapons and axe is his first weapon. Any sharp stone can be transformed into an axe and it also indicates the first settlement of humans in forests. The seventh incarnation of Lord Vishnu is Lord Ram. He is civilized and has developed more superior weapons like the bow and arrows. He has cleared the forests and developed small communities or villages. He is very vigilant and protects his villages and people. The eighth incarnation of Lord Vishnu is Lord Balarama. He is portrayed with the plough—the beginning of full-fledged cultivation. Human civilization has developed agriculture and is no longer dependent on meat and forest for food. It was the beginning of the agrarian economy. The ninth incarnation of Lord Vishnu is Krishna. He represents the advancing human civilization. He is associated with cows, the beginning of domestication of animals and development of economy, which continues to the present day. The tenth incarnation of Lord Vishnu is Kalki and is yet to arrive. He is believed to ride on a swift horse Devadatha and destroy the world. It is a clear indication that human beings will bring an end to life on earth. The numerous natural calamities created by human beings and the numerous nuclear weapons stored illustrate this.

Scientists from Leeds University have discovered that the world was ruled by pig-like creatures for a million years. The "Age of the Porcine" occurred around 260 million years ago—when the creatures called lystrosaurs were the few survivors of a mass extinction. Nearly 95 per cent of the living species were destroyed by a series of volcanic eruptions leaving behind pigs in a "golden age" of no predators.

They had Earth's abundant plant-life all to themselves. ""The remarkable thing about the lystrosaurs was their size." Nothing else that big seems to have got through the destruction – and that is why they were able to dominate Earth for so long. They fed and spread." We think there were billions of them. Their fossils are every where Lystrosaurs were similar in size to modern pigs, with snouts and small tusks for rooting around in vegetation.

Dasavatharam explains the stages of evolution of mankind. Matsya (Fish) Avatar being the first, explains living in water. The next Avatar was Tortoise which lived in water and land. Stage by stage he reached Parasuram stage using dagger and then Rama avatar using bow and arrow.

IMPORTANT VISHNU TEMPLES IN LANKA

VENAKETSHWARA VARATHARAJA PERUMAL VISHNU KOVIL

This temple is located in Kannathidy in Jaffna town. This temple was built in 1665 during Dutch period by the Chet ties. Unlike Portuguese, the Dutch did not do much destruction to Hindu temples.

VARATHARAJAH PERUMAL KOVIL PONNALAI

This temple is located near Moolai. An old Buddhist temple was discovered close to this temple. Historians are of the view that a Buddhist temple turned into the Vishnu temples. Another explanation is the link with Pallava Kingdom where Buddhism and Vaishnavisim thrived and traders introduced Vishnu temple in some coastal areas.

VALLIPURAM AALVAR TEMPLE — THUNAALAI.

Vallipuram is a part of Thunalai migrants from an area called Vallipuram in Namakkal Coimbatore settled in this and as such it must have got its name. Vallipuram (Sandy City) has a recorded history from the 2nd century BC, in the gold inscription of King Vasabha, where the local ruler is named as "Asagiri. Vallipuram (Sandy City) has a recorded history from the 2nd century BC, in the gold inscription of King Vasabha, where the local ruler is named as "Asagiri. Vallipuram has very rich archaeological remains that point at an early settlement. Between the 2nd and 12th centuries AD, the Cholas and Pallavas did extensive sea trade throughout Southeast Asia and China

The temple is surrounded by sand and has a long history behind it. A legend says that a Paravar lady

Vallinachi found a chakra in the sea and she built a temple for it considering it as symbol of Vishnu. The story is linked with Matcha avatar of Vishnu in connection with the sea. It would have been built by traders who came from the Pallava dynasty as Pallava's were Vishnu worshippers. The temple was a small hut during 15nth century. However by 1981 seventy one feet Raja Gopuram was built facing the east. There is a Ganesh temple in the west. Devotees worship him first before worshiping Vishnu. Three miles between the temple and the sea is covered by sand. People believed that Vishnu protected the temple and the village from the tidal waves of the sea.

According to some archeologist, before Nallur, Vallipuram was the Singai nagar. During the 2nd century BC gold inscription of King Vasabha was discovered in Vallipuram. Historians say that the descendents of Arya Chakravarti married into Kalinga Magha family and ruled from Vallipuram, one time popular port and re named it as Singai Nagar. Vallipuram Buddha statue was found in excavations proving the fact that traders from Pallava kingdom who were Buddhsits had influence in Vallipuram.

NEDUMAL VISHNU TEMPLE DEHIWALA

A 300-year "Nedumal" (Balaji) temple on the outskirts of Colombo has survived the ravages of Sri Lanka's turbulent times to emerge as a spiritual bridge between the Sinhalese & Tamils. The Vishnu-Nedumal is a symbol of the togetherness despite the deep divisions brought by the 25-year bloody ethnic war. "This temple has always attracted a large number of people from both communities and the numbers have increased tremendously in the past 20 years or so," says Narayana Potti, the senior priest of the temple who hailed from Tirunelveli in Tamil Nadu. Sinhalese, devout Buddhists by religion refer to the temple as "Vishnu-Kovil" and find themselves at home there as all the priests fluently converse in their language.

The temple, and its chief deity Lord Venkateswara, devoutly referred to by Tamils as "Nedumal" (Perumal in Tamil Nadu) whose statue was brought from Tirupati Andhra Pradesh, has acquired an immense popularity from the Temple's legendary history spanning over 300 years. The temple, according to its present records, was built by a Tamil civil contractor Theeran, who while attending to civic works of Dehiwala canal outside Colombo during the Dutch period in the 18th century heard a divine call. He stumbled on its ruins in the forests located a few kilometres away. It was first believed to have been discovered by an unknown devotee, who after a divine call, followed a mysterious calf into the forest which had vanished after leaving him at the place where he later discovered Sangu (the conch) and Chakram the wheel), which are always carried by Vishnu. Now the temple is called Mini-Tirupati as people who have no means and opportunity to visit Lord Perumal at Tirupati offer Him prayers at this temple.

*   *   *

16

Kannagi Amman (Pathini) Worship

The story of Kannagi happened in Madurai during first century AD. Manimekali and Silapathikarm were Sanga period literature. Manimegalai, according to the story was born daughter of Mathavi and Kovalan. She got interested in Buddhism. Later after learning doctrinal expositions from Buddhism, she became a dedicated Buddhist monk. The Chola King Uthayakumaran was madly in love with Manimegalai. He was a foolish king, who wanted everything thing to be done only in his way.

The King Gajabahu brought a statue of the Kannagi with the silampu (anklet) to Lanka. Legends of Kannagi Amman visiting various spots in the North and East of Lanka are passed down to generations by word of mouth. After his first stop in Sudumalai in Manipay, her next stop was Panrithalaichi Amman kovil also in Jaffna. She then visited the East of the island. In Batticaloa, she stopped at seven locations.

According to legend Kannagi came floating in a casket. The casket reached the shores of a place called Aaraiyampathy. She appeared in the dream of one teacher by the name of Sinnathamby, and told him, "My casket is on the shores of this village. Take that and set up a temple for me." Accordingly, that teacher went to the sea shore, found the casket, took the statue and with the help of the people built a temple with leaves.

This teacher being a farmer too, had gone to his field and while in the watch-hut fell asleep. Again, Kannagi Amman appeared in his dream and said, "Here I am getting wet in the rain while you are sleeping peacefully. Your paddy will be alright. Stop the roof from leaking." The teacher got up saw the paddy heaped after harvesting, and ran to the temple. He collected the men of the village and put up a stone structure for Kannagi Amman. He was worried as to who could perform the puja.

Again Kannagi Amman appeared in his dream and told one Panthan Kaddadi generation would conduct the puja, and so that family has been performing the puja from then on. The temple festival is in the Tamil month of May 15-June 15.

Besides Aaryampathy there are six other places which Kannagi Amman visited. Temples were constructed for her at Puthukudyyiruppu, Karainagar, Kokkatticholai and three other places. In all these places legend says miracles have taken place. People throng to the temple during the annual festival on full moon day in May, have 'Pongal (Boiling of rice and milk). Almost in all Kannagi temples these are the usual event — Cavadi, fire walking and other penances — to fulfil a vow.

After travelling in two places in Jaffna, seven places in Batticaloa, Mullaitivu was selected as the 10th place for the temple. Originally it was 'Paththam Pallai' (Paththam — tenth; Pallai — resting place). In the course of time it has turned out to be Vattapalai. In Vattappalai too she appeared in person to some shepherd boys, as an old woman. When a Portuguese General wanted to destroy the temple, an old lady shook the Panicham tree near the temple and chased away the soldier.

According to legend she had asked them to put up a hut for her. Later she asked them to light a lamp. When the boys told her there was no oil, she told them to get the sea water, and use it like oil. This tradition continues to this day. In all the ten places where she stopped, she had performed some miracle or other.

In Hinduism, each deity has a favourite tree. Amman prefers the Neem tree (herbal tree). At many of these stop-over, she is said to have sat on a dead fallen trunk of the Neem tree and it had sprouted to life.

At Vattappalai, she asked the shepherds to look for lice in her head. And when the children did so, they saw the head full of eyes — they got frightened she disappeared.

Dead scared these children ran to the village with the news of this strange visitor. When the village folk went running back here, she was not there.

They knew it was Amman, and since she had eyes (Kann in Tamil) on her head they assumed it must be Kannagi Amman. That was how Kannagi temple was built at that very spot. Whether in Jaffna, Vanni or Batticaloa, Kannagi Amman temples appeared due to Amman appearing in person or in the dreams of ardent devotees whether it is a king or a beggar.

Thus in Lanka there were many worshipping places of Kannagi Amman. In these places legend and folklore play an important part and not history, in practising Kannagi worship.

Kannagi was strong in her chastity. At her age of marriage, her parents married to a merchant named Kovalan. He was play boy and got interested in the temple dancer Madhavi. Kovalan separated from Kannagi and lived with Madhavi and Manimegalai was born to them. Kannagi had no children but still loved the husband. Kovalan spent all his wealth on Madhavi and returned to Kannagi penniless. When Kovalan asked for money from Kannagi to start a new life, she removed one of her anklets and gave it Kovalan to sell, make money and start a business. He sold the anklet to the palace jeweller who had stolen the Queens anklet. The king wanted people to find the anklet. The jeweller falsely accused Kovalan of stealing the anklet. The king without proper inquiry made a mistake and ordered Kovalan to be beheaded. Hearing about the death of the husband, Kannagi went to the King and accused him for wrongly ordering the execution of her husband. Her anger was so intense that the King got scared. She proved to the king that her anklet was different from the queen's one. The King realised his mistake. Kannagi cursed the kingdom, her chastity bestowed power to command the elements and she burnt the city of Mathurai. Kannagi was upset and sad over the destruction of the city of Madurai, left the place and went to Sera Nadu. She died there after her husband's death between AD 113-135. Sera king Sengutuvan's brother Illango adigal, a Buddhist monk wrote the story of Kannagi as the famous epic Silapathigaram.

King Senguttuvan went to the Himalayas, brought a stone and made a statue of Kannagi for worship because of the great respect for her. Between the periods 171 to 193 AD king Gajabahu who ruled from Anuradhapura went to Sera Kingdom to attend the festival organised by Sengutuvan for Kannagi. The festival made Gajabahu to respect and surprised at the wonders of Kannagi. He brought a similar statue to Lanka through Mathagal in Jambukolam port and established several temples for Kannagai on the way to Anuradhapura. The Kannagi Amman temple in Mullaitivu was the tenth one and hence is called Vattapalai Amman temple. Similar to the festival for Kannagi, at the Perahera in Kandy, Kannagi by the name of Pathini amman was carried in procession. Several temples were constructed in Sinhalese areas in the south and eastern provinces. There is a list of Sinhalese villages where Pathini temples were constructed namely Dedigama, Maduwa Pattini Devale — Kandy — Medagoda (Sitawake), Nawagamuwa Devale — is said to be built by king Rajasingha I (1581-1593).This is situated in Colombo closer to the Avissawella Low level road. It is the principal cult centre for worship of the Goddess. Panama — 15Km South of Arugam Bay Ratnapura Seeni Gama (Hikaduwa) Wibawa (Kurunegala), Kabulumulla Kannagi Amman worship became popular in the Eastern province. Kannagi Amman temple gradually became Rajeswary Amman temple. During the 16th century AD Kannagi worship became popular in the Batticaloa area. Small kings in Eastern province spread this worship. During the Portuguese period Veddah caste people migrated to Batticaloa district. A person by the name Kandappar brought seven Kannagi Amman statues and established in the eastern province and people started worship. During 2nd century AD, the statue of Senpagaselvi was established in Thambuluvilla and worshiped. From 2nd century AD until 12th century AD Kannagi worship flourished in the Eastern province. To get rain in the area, the popular Kombu (horn) game in Kannagi story was practised.

Singhalese and Tamils believed that by worshiping Kannagi Amman, all infectious diseases could be cured. People use Margossa (Neem) leaves as herbal cure for chicken pox, measles etc.

ANGANAKADAVAI KANNAGI AMMAN TEMPLE.

The first Kannagi Amman temple was established in the Jaffna peninsular at Anganakadavai. Angana refers to Amman. During the Dutch period, the temple was destroyed and reconstructed again. Anganammai refers to Kannagi. The statue of Kannagi was brought to Mathagal port and the temple would have been established in this area closer to the port. The temple is located west of Kandarodai. It was established in 2nd Century BC. In the past, people who travel from Mathagal pass Anganakadavai temple on their way to Kandarodai.

VATTAPALAI KANNAGI AMMAN TEMPLE

Vattapalai Kannagi Amman temple is considered as the guardian God of Vanni area. The village Vattapalai is located closer to Mulliyavallai, Thanniyutru in Mullaithivu area. There are legendary stories about this temple. On the day of the pongal this water is brought to the Amman Temple in the morning and a lamp is lit with the sea water instead of oil and it keeps burning the whole day and night This temple lies three miles off the main road leading to Mullaitivu among swaying coconut palms. Legend has it that after the consecration of the shrine of Kannagi in South India, the deity visited Ceylon manifesting herself in 10 places where temples were built for the Goddess. This last or the tenth place was Paththam Palai (Paththam means tenth, Palai — means residence). During the course of time the name has changed to Vattapalai.

The Brahmin priest blesses the event. The person who starts the pongal sits in front of the fireplace and takes the pot on to his lap and using twine thread makes a network of it covering the pot, when this is done, the temple stewards take the pot and he stands up and receives it. Thereafter he goes into a trance, going round the fire place with the pot balanced precariously on one shoulder.

As he dances around the fire place supported by the stewards, some rice grains are put into his out stretched hand and he throws the grains upwards in each direction. When we asked the reason for this, we were told that the grains are for the celestial companions of the Amman. Believe it or not even one grain didn't fall on the ground or on anybody's head for that matter. Once he puts the pot on the fireplace the man becomes normal. This happens at midnight and milk rice sweetened with jaggery is cooked. As soon as the main pongal starts, devotees who have vowed to cook milk rice there, start their minor pongal in the sandy compound. Fire walking and kavadi also take place there.

This temple too has a history of miracles. A person with plundering intention had his eyes on the precious jewels of the deity had gone there. He went to the hall where the pilgrims rest to see if anyone was around. The assistant of the priest was asleep there with a shawl covering his body. The prowler took the shawl and was on his way into one of the wadiyas built for carpenters. He then took off his shirt and hooked it on the fence, buried his wrist watch in the sand and made his way to the temple. He used the camphor to light the place. He made quick work of it and keeping the box of jewels on the wall below the cave, came to the hut. As soon as he reached the wadiya he was struck blind. Later he is believed to have confessed that something white went over his eyes and he lost his sight, needless to say that when he was discovered with the shawl what would have happened to him. People came flooding to see the thief. There was general excitement over the miraculous deed of the Amman and the faith of devotees grew stronger.

During the time the Portuguese controlled the area, people say that a certain General used to mock and deride the devotees going to the temple. 'Can your Goddess perform miracles like our Lady of Miracles', he would taunt them. One day when he was riding past the temple arrogantly, a tree which they call Anickia Tree — which was beside the wall of the sanctum sanctorum of the temple, shook so violently that the fruits from the tree fell down and pelted the general till he fell off the horse. It is said that to this day after that incident, the tree bore neither a flower nor a fruit.

NAAGAPOOSANI AMMAN TEMPLE IN THE ISLAND OF NAINATHEEVU

Naagapoosani Amman Kovil is an ancient Sakthi temple in Naina-theevu ("theevu" means island), off Jaffna peninsula, famous for both its historical background as well as people's devotion. The island is called as Manipallavam. The name of the island alludes to its aboriginal inhabitants, the Naka people off shoot from Kerala. They worshiped snakes. Historians note the island is mentioned in the ancient Tamil sangam literature and ancient Buddhist legends of Sri Lanka such as Mahavamsa.

According to historians, there stood a temple of magnificent stone structure at this site for several centuries worshiped by people from both Jaffna region and nearby Tamil kingdoms of Southern India, which was destroyed by the Portuguese colonial invaders (with the fall of Jaffna Kingdom) during the second decade of 17th century A.D. The present temple was built in stages by Hindus from Jaffna region after the successive Portuguese and Dutch Colonials powers, which deprived religious freedom of the local people, left the country. This temple has link with Buddhism as Manimegalai daughter of Kovalan who turned into Buddhist nun, visited the temple.

* * *

17

Guardian deities in Sri Lanka

GUARDIAN DEITIES

In Tamil Nadu guardian deities are many. They differ from village to village and worshiped based on different beliefs. In Lanka, the most commons are Ayyanar, Vyravar, Maha Kali Amman, and Mari Amman.

The farmers who live in Vanni and Anuradhapura areas depend on their living on land and water and the rain. They accumulated the water in the tanks and used the water during dry season. In order to prevent the tank and land being not destroyed by floods, the farmers considered Aynor as the guardian deity. There are many Aiyanar temples appearing near the bunds of the tanks. They did pujas for aiyanar to bless them with rain. The guardian of Minneriya tank is Minneriya god, Kalu (Black) god, Bairava god and many such Guardian gods. Many rituals are adopted in doing Puja for these deities to ensure harvesting is done successfully. Between Lord Shiva and Vishnu Aiyanar worshiping appeared.

Ayyappan's origin is uncertain, but is sometimes believed to be an incarnation of Dharma Sastra, who is the offspring of Shiva and Vishnu (as Mohini, in his female form). In Lanka, white elephant is considered as the vehicle for Aiyanar. In the islands in Jaffna peninsula, there are many Aiyanar temples in the sea coast. There are many stories linking Vediarasan, Poothathambi with Aiyanar. Analaitheevu Aiyyanar. The temple was very old and was demolished by Portuguese. Many Hindu temples in Sri Lanka were demolished during Portuguese rule.

Vairavar is called **Bhairava** ("Terrible" or "Frightful") sometimes known as **Vairavar** (In Tamil), is the fierce manifestation of Lord Shiva associated with annihilation.[2] He is one of the most important deities of Rajasthan, Tamil Nadu, Lanka and Nepal. He is depicted ornamented with a range of twisted serpents, which serve as earrings, bracelets, anklets, and sacred thread He wears a tiger skin and a ritual apron composed of human bones. Bhairava has a dog as his divine vehicle. Bhairava himself has eight manifestations: Kala Bhairava, Asitanga Bhairava, Samhara Bhairava, Rudra Bhairava, Krodha Bhairava, Kapala Bhairava, Rudra Bhirava and Unmatta Bhairava. Kala Bhairava is conceptualized as the Guru of the planetary deity Saturn.

BATHIRAKALI AMMAN TEMPLE MUNEESWARAM

Pathirakali Amman is the guardian deity for Muneeswaram. The cult of Kali reached Sri Lanka via South India. Although Kali shrines may have been part of Tamil Hindu temples prior to 12th century CE, the Sinhalese Buddhist population came to revere Kali as a village demon at least by the 12th century CE. The first known Hindu temple with a shrine to Kali to become popular with the Sinhalese Buddhists is Muneeswaram. A myth that has Kali landing at the town of Chilaw, and residing in Muneeswaram, has made the temple a popular place of visit for cursing and sorcery purposes. In the early 1970s, the majority of the Sinhalese visitors were there for sorcery purposes, but by 1990s more than half have been visiting the temple for general veneration purposes, demonstrating the transformation of the deity from a malevolent demigod to a mother goddess. Since 1960s a number of Sinhalese Buddhist shrines dedicated to Kali have sprung up all over the island, especially in urban areas. These are managed by Sinhalese priests who are trance specialists and act as intermediaries between the deity and the devotee while being posses by the deity.

There are many interesting stories about this temple. Animal and bids were sacrificed as a vow in this temple.

Recently, due to political involvement, the sacrifice is stopped. The appearance of the deity looks fearful.

Sudalai Maadan, is a regional Tamil male deity popular in Thoothukudi Tamil Nadu, He is considered to be the son of Shiva and Parvati and. He seems to have originated in some ancestral guardian spirit of the villages or communities in Tamil Nadu, in a similar manner as Ayyanar.

Maadan's principal role is being a protector and a hero (Veeran). He is the divinity of the dispossessed. Madan is usually considered to be the caste deity of the Naidu, Pillai, Pallar, Konar, Thevar. Pariyar, Nadar and other castes. This deity is very popular in the southern districts. Large Madan temples are rare. Madan shrines usually consist of simple stone platforms with stone pillars. They are usually located at the outskirts of the villages. Sometimes Madan is painted on the pillar and sometimes he is represented in sculpture form, but frequently those pillars are only white, daubed with red marks. When Madan is represented ichnographically, he is usually standing in a threatening position, carrying weapons (Sickle, club, sword, cleaver, whip) in both hands. Owing to the non-Vedic origin of this deity, rituals in most Madan temples are officiated by non-Brahmin priests. Each Caste or families will have their own Madan temple in their villages. This worship is not popular in

Lanka as caste system is not predominant. The deity exhibits bravery, and goes out for hunting.

NAGATHAMBIRAN TEMPLE.

Worshiping snake is common in Tamil Nadu and Lanka. Naga worshiping started 3500 years ago in the Indus valley civilization. Vishnu is linked to serpent. Naga worship is popular in Kerala. In Lanka, naga temples exist in Mankulam, Puliyankulam, Mulliavalai, Vanni areas. A female naga is a Nagi. The Snake primarily represents rebirth, death and mortality, due to its casting of its skin and being symbolically "reborn".

CONCLUSION:

Hinduism contains many legendary stories based on the concepts of the religion. The stories were written over a long period of time and turned into ritual process in some temples. The stories teach a lesson in the way of living. Some are popular epics such as Ramayana, Mahabaratha. With time, Hinduism may undergo transformation in its philosophy. In Sri Lanka Hinduism is interlaced with Buddhism. In Pereharas like in Kandy, Thondeswaram, Hindu deity plays an important part. The Buddha's relation with Hinduism is so close that it's easy to confuse Buddhism with Hinduism. The two religions have close connections, and yet they are distinct. This was because of Buddha's reform movements and his refining of Hindu beliefs. It would not be wrong to state, then, that Buddha founded a noble religion by distilling Hinduism, and offering a commonsense approach to self-betterment to which the people can relate easily. Hindu devotees should look back at science and nature and interpret it with the beliefs in Hinduism. Laws of nature are intermingled with Hinduism.

*   *   *

Acknowledgement

The author of the book thanks those who provided the images in the book. He is grateful to Artist Pugalenthy (Kannan) from Ontario Canada, Photographer Devaka Seneviratne from Colombo, Sri Lanka and for Mr Selvakumar of **www.nselva.com**, www.mathagal.com, www.uoctamil.com for giving permission to publish the images of Thiruketheeswaram temple and Vallipuram temple (Gopuram) and Selvasannathi temple.